Gothic Grimoire

About the Author

Konstantinos has a bachelor's degree in journalism and technical writing and is a published author of articles and short fiction. This is his fifth book published by Llewellyn. He is also the author of *Vampires: The Occult Truth, Summoning Spirits: The Art of Magical Evocation, Contact the Other Side: 7 Methods for Afterlife Communication,* and *Nocturnal Witchcraft: Magick After Dark.*

A Dark Neopagan, Konstantinos has been researching the occult and practicing magick for over fifteen years. He is also a trained stage mentalist who uses these skills to debunk fraudulent affectations of the supernatural. Konstantinos often lectures on paranormal topics at bookstores and colleges. He also devotes time to singing Gothic rock music, and to exploring nocturnal life both in New York City and around the country.

To Write to the Author

If you wish to contact the author or would like more information about this book, please write to the author in care of Llewellyn Worldwide and we will forward your request. Both the author and publisher appreciate hearing from you and learning of your enjoyment of this book and how it has helped you. Llewellyn Worldwide cannot guarantee that every letter written to the author can be answered, but all will be forwarded. Please write to:

Konstantinos
℅ Llewellyn Worldwide
P.O. Box 64383, Dept. 0-7387-0255-2
St. Paul, MN 55164-0383, U.S.A.
Please enclose a self-addressed stamped envelope for reply,
or $1.00 to cover costs. If outside U.S.A., enclose
international postal reply coupon.

Many of Llewellyn's authors have websites with additional
information and resources. For more information,
please visit our website at
http://www.llewellyn.com

Gothic Grimoire

KONSTANTINOS

2002
Llewellyn Publications
St. Paul, Minnesota 55164-0383, U.S.A.

First Edition
Second Printing, 2002

Author photo by David Armstrong
Book design by Donna Burch
Cover design by Kevin R. Brown
Editing by Karin Simoneau

ISBN 0-7387-0255-2

Konstantinos, 1972–
    Gothic grimoire / Konstantinos.
        p.   cm.
    ISBN 0-7387-0255-2
    I. Magic. 2. Night—Miscellanea. I. Title

    BF1611 .K66 2002
    133.4'3—dc21   2002075501

Llewellyn Worldwide does not participate in, endorse, or have any authority or responsibility concerning private business transactions between our authors and the public.

All mail addressed to the author is forwarded but the publisher cannot, unless specifically instructed by the author, give out an address or phone number.

Any Internet references contained in this work are current at publication time, but the publisher cannot guarantee that a specific location will continue to be maintained. Please refer to the publisher's website for links to authors' websites and other sources.

Llewellyn Publications
A Division of Llewellyn Worldwide, Ltd.
P.O. Box 64383, Dept. 0-7387-0255-2
St. Paul, MN 55164-0383, U.S.A.
www.llewellyn.com

Other Books by Konstantinos

Vampires: The Occult Truth

Summoning Spirits: The Art of Magical Evocation

Contact the Other Side: 7 Methods for Afterlife Communication

Nocturnal Witchcraft: Magick After Dark

'Tis the good reader that makes the good book

Ralph Waldo Emerson
American lecturer, poet and essayist 1803-1882

Contents

Warning!

Some of the advanced rituals in this book will require the use of fire and even your blood, and may bring you into contact with powerful emotional forces. Neither the publisher nor the author will be held responsible for the misuse of these workings.

Proceed with caution.

Introduction

How to Use this Tome

I've got a feeling that if you're reading this book, it found you. Not the other way around. Some of us belong in the shadows, and are drawn by the nocturnal mysteries.

This is the first advanced book of Witchcraft that is dedicated to a dark, yet positive, current. A Book of Shadows from the shadows, indeed. And like a Book of Shadows or traditional grimoire, it assumes certain knowledge on the part of the reader.

As promised in *Nocturnal Witchcraft: Magick After Dark* (Llewellyn, 2002), this grimoire takes what was taught in the other book much farther. In the other, I cover how to tap into the energies of night—how to call the Dark Gods and Goddesses and assume their godforms, cast circles attuned to darkness, skry dark surfaces for visions, work with psychic energy, and even read minds. However, if you're not new to the Craft, you should be able to apply most of your own ritualistic techniques to make the rites in this grimoire work, possibly with the exception of the advanced mind-reading techniques (to work with those,

I strongly recommend you check out the unique basics covered in *Nocturnal Witchcraft*, even if you only borrow a copy to read the chapters on mind reading).

So, when you encounter a line such as "cast a magick circle," it will be your call as to what to do. The same goes for lines such as "achieve some inner quiet," "raise emotional energy," "skry," and "invoke the God/dess." Either apply the basics of the Craft of Night as I taught them, or rely on the techniques that have worked for you before. That's the key to the occult, really—apply what works for you!

And now, on to what awaits you within these pages. Everything included works, you'll find, because night is tangible—it is an ether of sorts. This ether does more than just embrace us when we step out into it. It carries magickal energy, and the voices of the Dark Gods and Goddesses. The night is a quieter psychic time, free of the hectic energies of the day. As those in your area begin to settle down for sleep, banishing all analytical thought, the psychic ether becomes quieter—an interference-free realm in which you can create dark miracles.

How can I sound so sure that you'll be creating changes in the universe worthy of the miracle moniker? Because that's how I perceived these mystical wonders, and I figure if they work for me, there's no reason they shouldn't work for you just as well, if not better. I wasn't born with any special abilities—just a love of things dark, and a curiosity to make the energies of the unseen work for me.

A great deal of the rites and techniques found in these pages have never seen publication in any form, and will be, I hope, perfect companions to your own Book of Shadows.

You will find here nocturnal ways of celebrating the Sabbats. Prepare to explore the dark ether firsthand by leaving your body with a foolproof method. Expand your intuition and even learn a way to read tarot that will change forever the way you look at the cards—literally. Along with these and dozens of other dark delights, you will learn how to break down the gates to the Underworld, either coming face to face with the dead, or with your own dark half.

Welcome to a treatise on night's own special kind of magick . . . for those night claims as its own.

Part One

Living the
Nocturnal Tradition

Chapter One

Stepping into the Current

Your way of life can never be truly codified by others. Seeker of dark mysteries, how you choose to fulfill your desires shall always be flexible. Yet perhaps you've begun to notice that in your exploration of the dark side of the occult, you're experiencing something that is much more than just a collection of nocturnal experiments.

There is a very tangible current or energy at work in the ether of night. If this is your first foray into nocturnal magick, then maybe you still need some time to feel the current. But even after invoking just a few dark gods and goddesses, and tapping into the ether of night for inspiration, it is almost impossible to not feel that the darkness possesses just such a current—an energy that seeks to embrace and carry you along to the accomplishment of greater things.

This dark current is, in a way, the only ally you need in your path to spiritual development. It links you to the Source through the guise of the nocturnal deities. It gives you, this energy you can tap into, the tools you need to transform reality around you.

Learn here, in Part One, how to use this current to fully step into the night's mysteries.

Identifying the Nocturnal Tradition

In Witchcraft, a new energy current usually forms around a new tradition. Some High Priest or Priestess determines a set of practices and rites, deities and myths, to base a tradition upon. Practitioners then give energy to the whole, adding vitality to the new current being formed. All Wiccan traditions have begun in this way.

Contrary to popular legend, there are no Wiccan covens with lineages dating back hundreds of years. While Paganism is many thousands of years old, it was never celebrated in quite the way that Witches do so now. This is why many Witches prefer to add a prefix to their theology, calling it Neopaganism. Traditions are relatively new, be they the ones Gerald Gardner or Alex Sanders began last century, or any of the others that followed. Again, until now, Wiccan traditions would come first, then an energy current would form around them.

The current of night, however, has always been here. How can I or any other Witch ever claim to have created this current? Dark power has always existed, and has been tapped by countless magick users through the years. The Nocturnal Tradition, therefore, is one we must attempt to identify in reverse, if you will. It is a tradition formed to make best use of a timeless force that has shown itself to nightkind each sunset for millennia.

While I am presenting here rites that will enable you to live year-round within something I'm identifying as the Nocturnal Tradition, the rites can ultimately be molded to meet your needs. This tradition is what you nightkind make of it, after all. You can use the practices presented here, as they are, for decades, or you can immediately rewrite them—I won't mind. The night's energy is still there, waiting to be tapped. I only hope to help you feel its reality and make practical use of this current.

Initiation

If you've performed any kind of self-dedication to the God and Goddess and have begun working with dark magick, then you have experienced the dark current. A few short lunar cycles after said dedication, you should have felt that your connection to the universe expanded. If you've only just begun working with magick, you'll soon know what I mean.

Everything starts to seem different when you walk down a magickal path. In magick, results are obtained when probabilities and coincidences are bent slightly to ultimately provide you with what you ask for. Do a spell for a new car, and you may either get a raise to make possible the payments on a new car, or may even win one in a contest. The universe decides how results are obtained.

Well, coincidences and bending probabilities and the like abound even when you're not waiting for a set magickal result. This is because life itself is a path toward a magickal result—toward adepthood or occult mastery. Working with a current sets this all in motion. Even newly developed currents take on a form of tangible intelligence in time, providing the universe with a means of helping you. A current as old as that of night, however, can powerfully alter your life.

To more fully allow yourself to be swept up by the wonderful gifts awaiting you in the darkness, you should consider taking your dedication a level further through full initiation. Contrary to legend—and recent legend, at that—you can initiate yourself. Again, there are no centuries-old traditions that can claim the authority to pass on a figurative torch. And even in ancient days, when Paganism was the prevalent religion of most lands for millennia, self-initiation rites still existed, ranging from inner vision quests to dangerous exposures to the elements in the wild.

The Self-Initiation found here will only strengthen your link to the unseen world and to the night itself. Think of the night as an ether filled with intent—a viscous intelligence that closes in on you with each passing sunset. In time, the dark will guide you where you need to go with gentle nudges or even startling pushes in the right direction.

Initiation allows this current to carry you in the fullest sense of what the word "current" implies.

In addition to helping your development, the Self-Initiation will strengthen your link to Divinity. The gods and goddesses of night will somehow feel closer to you from the moment you complete the rite. This is no hallucination on your part. The dark current is what you use to access these deities. By aligning yourself more closely with the dark current, you allow your soul a freer way to reach the godforms built upon the same energy.

To perform this ritual, you will need an altar that is fully set up. Make sure there is a black skrying device or "nocturnal portal" on the center. You will also need to cast either a nocturnal circle or whatever magick circle you're comfortable with.

In addition, a couple of extra items will be necessary. One is a lidless black box about the size of a shoebox. This can literally be the latter, covered on the outside with black construction paper or paint. The box will be used upside down as a cover for some items that you need to place at the foot of the altar.

These items? For starters, you'll need a piece of obsidian. This can be of any size, but consider that it will be something you keep around for a long time, so make sure it's a piece you like.

Also, gather representations of the four elements that make sense to you. A feather for air, perhaps, or some rocks for earth? How about a match for fire and a shell for water? Don't worry too much about what you select. Unlike the obsidian, these representations of the elements will not be around with you for long at all and should be disposable.

This next item is one you don't have much leeway with. You need to find some kind of small toy human skull, unless you happen to have a real human one lying around (and if so, I don't need to know why!). Odd as this sounds, trust me on the skull's necessity for now.

The last item is a one-sided hand mirror. Place this facedown on the ground before your altar and put the other objects on top of the mirror. Try to arrange the objects so that the elemental symbols are toward the appropriate quarters on the mirror, and place the skull in the center. The skull should be facing west (and all the objects should be on the floor to the west of the altar, where you normally stand). Behind or to the east of the skull, place the piece of obsidian. It should not be visible if you kneel before the items on the floor.

Cover the objects with the overturned black box and prepare yourself for the Self-Initiation. Before you undertake this powerful transformation rite, however, be certain to read through it a couple of times, even visualizing how you'll carry it out. It contains a few steps that are more dramatic than the typical ritual and which you'll perform much easier after having imagined them.

Self-Initiation Rite

Take a ritual bath if possible, imagining that you are being purified by the water around you.

Do a self-relaxation meditation or rite.

Cast a magick circle, but do not invoke the God or Goddess yet.

Place both palms on the altar and kneel before it, being careful not to knock over the black box with your knees.

Spend a moment feeling a connection with the energy present in your altar. Your palms may start tingling.

Look into the nocturnal portal until you can see your reflection. Think about how you coexist with the glowing darkness around you, and about how your life has been changing as a result. Think of your first successful invocation, your first manifested thoughtform or spell result.

Gaze into the reflection of your eyes and say:

I now delve deeper into the shadows.
May the gods and goddesses of night guide their still-blind child
on the road of the seeker.
So mote it be.

Move your face back from the portal, seeing its reflection blend fully with the darkness.

Lift your hands and wave into your face some of the incense smoke that you used to cast your circle. Close your eyes and let the mystical scent alter your mood and, ultimately, your state of mind.

Stand up suddenly and move clockwise around the altar to the east. If you feel a head rush, however, pause for a moment before making such a move. When at the east, say:

I now depart the land of the rising sun for the realms of darkness.
Whoever dies shall be reborn.

Now, move *counter*clockwise to the west of the circle and, as dramatically as you can, simulate your own death. Bizarre as it sounds, you should face the west and collapse (carefully!) to the ground, without losing view of the west until after you've hit the ground. When you do complete your simulated collapse, slowly close your eyes.

Against the black backdrop of your mind's eye, imagine that before you, to the west, there is a pair of glowing silver columns. Crackling all around them is silver lightning. Try to hear this lightning. Try to feel its pulsing, its static tingling all over your body. For this is the only thing you can feel—your body is otherwise numb.

Focus on the silver pillars. Note how the lightning cannot touch these columns, bouncing away each time it gets close to them. And the lightning is slowly disappearing from your mind's-eye field of vision. See, the silver columns are moving apart.

Imagine that you are moving closer to this dark abyss between the columns. What do you see there? Skry this gate of the west, this land of the dead. What impressions do you receive from this realm? Symbolically, the self that you used to be proud of being is now dead. A new, darker identity is being born within you. Allow any impressions and visions to come to you, but do not worry about their meanings just yet. You can dwell on them later.

Feel yourself pulling back suddenly from this gate of the west. Immediately open your eyes and stand up as quickly as possible. Pause for a moment to let yourself become oriented.

Move clockwise three times around the circle. Each time you pass the east, say:

I seek the guidance of the Dark Ones.
May the primary energy filling my life be that of night.

Feel the energy rising from your clockwise movements. After the last time you pass the east, return clockwise to the point before your altar. Drop to your knees instantly, feeling the energy releasing out of every inch of your body. This energy is rising up above.

Grab the black box before you. Close your eyes. Then, lift the box and throw it with force over your head so that it will be tossed behind you out of the circle.

Open your eyes and gaze upon the objects resting on the back of the mirror. Reach over the skull and past the visually hidden obsidian to pick up the air item. Say:

Intellect can only increase in the dark initiate.

Place the air item up on the altar without leaving your kneeling position. Reach back down and pick up the fire object. Say:

And the fires bring energy to the blackness that surrounds them,
to the initiate in whom they blaze.

Put the fire item on the altar without looking, but ensure that the object makes contact with the air item. These objects and the ones that will follow should begin to form a pile on the altar. Reach down to pick up the water item from the floor. Say:

More than the gate of death,
the west brings passion to whomever passes through.

Without looking up, place the water item on the altar, against the other two objects you put there. From the floor, lift the earth item. Say:

Buried within the dark mother's womb we await more
than new life—we seek existence with stability.

Put the earth item on the altar to complete the elemental pile resting there. Do not look at this pile yet, however. Reach down behind the skull and pick up the obsidian with your receiving hand (the opposite of your writing hand). Gaze into its darkness, saying:

May the elements be absorbed by you, creature of darkest stone.
May your reflective surface capture the elemental essences
as the black ether houses these forces each night.

Look up to the altar and see the elemental pile of symbols. Note how they are not exactly aligned with their compass directions. They are mixed, their energies intermingling. Try to imagine yellow, red, blue, and green energies swirling about the pile.

Thrust your receiving hand, which holds the obsidian, into the pile of the elemental objects. It's okay if they fall over or even off the altar. Make this thrusting movement with intensity. Imagine that the stone is absorbing into itself the present elemental forces. See the colors begin to move into and around the black stone.

Close your eyes. Keeping your receiving hand and the stone amidst the disrupted pile of objects, take a deep breath, imagining that the raw elemental energy present is coursing from the stone up into your receiving arm. Try your best to see the colors swirling about your arm. When you exhale, imagine the sensation and colors spreading throughout your body.

Repeat the drawing in of elemental energy twice more, imagining the color mists passing through you.

With reverence, gently position the obsidian on the altar before your nocturnal portal.

Return to a kneeling position before the one remaining object on top of the mirror on the floor. Look down at the skull.

Meditate on the powerful skull symbol for a few minutes. Allow even the wildest impressions to form. Some see the skull as a reminder of how fragile we are. An initiate sees a reminder that magick can animate even something as crude as this. Our lives are mystical experiences—experiences we repeat after coming face to face with the stage of life the skull also represents.

Before being given the gift of this incarnation by the God and Goddess, you had been decaying bones left over from another life.

Say:

That which dies shall be reborn.

Flip the mirror suddenly, knocking over the skull and replacing the bony face with a view of your own reflected face. Say:

I am prepared to animate the dead—to bring life to all magickal endeavors.

Stand before the altar and do an invocation of the universal aspect of either the God or Goddess of Night, your choice. However, for such a rite, do not call on a particular deity name. Just pick the gender you intuitively feel should be present with you this night, and call the universal form of him or her using these words or ones to a similar effect:

God/dess of Night, whose face is accented by the stars,
God/dess of Night, who embodies the dark ether about me,
be with me as I begin new life.
Surrounded by the elements of your creation,
I fully give myself to the dark current.
Armed with a growing awareness of reality,
I am prepared to see the unseen moving about me.
Be with me so that I may know my true will.

Allow a full godform assumption to happen (if you know how to do this), visualizing whatever the purest ideal of a nocturnal deity means to you. The God or Goddess may have some insight to share with you —be open to receive such wisdom.

When you feel the current begin to subside, you will be ready to close the circle and give thanks to the energies of the four quarters.

As with most Witchy workings, you can have at the end of your initiation a cake and ale ceremony (or "cake and drink," as I like to call it—who has ale these days?). The way you partake in this can be as elaborate as you wish, but do make sure to at least reflect how important this night is to you.

After the ceremony has ended, you should bury the four elemental representations you used, as well as the skull. Keep the obsidian in a safe place or carry it with you from time to time. It can act as a special reminder of your link to darkness on even the sunniest day. Look at it whenever you feel the need to be reminded of your initiation and powerful link to the current of night.

Congratulations, Nocturnal Witch, and welcome to the dark fold. Life will never be the same again.

I promise.

Chapter Two

Alone in the Dark or
Surrounded by Nightkind?

To be in a coven or not? From the 1950s to the 1980s—the early years of Wicca—it was considered not only important to be in a coven, but mandatory. You weren't a Witch unless you were initiated into an allegedly centuries-old tradition. Adhering to such fantastical guidelines, however, meant that no one could become a Witch!

Again, there are no centuries-old traditions. Don't be fooled by claims that some lineage is ancient and has survived to the present day. The Old Religion is an apt phrase for describing Paganism, *not* Wicca. The term Witchcraft has evolved from its lowercase *w* form to now act as a label for both religion and magick, making it the word I prefer to use more often than Wicca. Witchcraft is primal and all-encompassing, just like the word Pagan.

Being a Witch or Pagan does not require joining an existing organization. Since the earliest days, Paganism, light or dark, has been about humankind's connections to divinity. Some versions of Paganism, including most traditions of Wicca, have emphasized nature as a link to these higher forces. Nocturnal Witchcraft finds the way to deity in the shadows. Simple distinctions; however, all forms of Paganism can be performed alone.

The Gods and Goddesses do not ignore the call of a solitary any more than they give special attention to covens. Be assured, your link to the dark current will not be affected by your decision to work alone or with others. Like all aspects of life, though, certain benefits and drawbacks apply to letting others into your immediate sphere, so to speak.

The Solitary Shadow

What is it like to move as a solitary shadow through each magickal night of your development?

You tell me. Chances are you've been doing it for years. I know I have. I've belonged to both ceremonial lodges and poorly organized Pagan "circles," but the majority of my seeking has been done alone. The universe, the gods, the dark current—all these forces have a way of sending the right books and teachers into your life when you need them. But these guides that appear, be they human or bound paper, have a way of disappearing, too. Teachers run out of lessons, and books can be outgrown or out-mastered (one of the reasons that we authors keep writing new ones!).

Teachers and, indeed, most types of people come in and out of our lives. We are the true constants. Do seek companionship, but don't base your spiritual development on it. When we deal with covens in a moment, you'll see that my take on their importance is that they can be a useful thing for a time, but . . . well, we'll get to that.

All the techniques of Nocturnal Witchcraft that I teach can be performed alone. The years of criticizing solitaries have long since passed. It's never been easier to be a solitary Witch, and, as a result, the ranks of Witches have marvelously grown.

Remember that the most important thing to commune with is the gods and your own nature. Perform Dark and Full Moon rites, either ones you get from books or ones you write, and perform them monthly if possible. Try to do some form of celebration of the Sabbats, either the rites you're about to learn in the next chapter or ones you create. These actions will help keep you in sync with the energies surrounding you.

Then extend your interaction with magick to your daily life. Learn what you can from the night, from its inspiration. Apply your experience.

Using whatever technique works for you, do listen to the night. Do meditate during the dark hours and allow impressions to come to you. Doing so can be thought of as a major part of your daily "gospel" exposure. Inspiration by night can teach you things about yourself and how you can interact with the world while remaining true to your goals.

Leading a normal daytime life while being a Witch of the night is probably easiest when you're a solitary. There are no meetings to squeeze in, and no others who might blow your cover, so to speak. Likewise, if you choose to be public about your way of life, your solitary status makes it easier to do so, as you won't be exposing any in-the-broom-closet coven members through association.

On the topic of your public status, that's something only you can determine. Witchcraft is becoming more accepted each year. However, being a Witch of any form or tradition is still not the easiest thing to reveal to parents, or certain coworkers, or teachers, or anyone whose reaction might have a negative effect on your life. Again, listen to the night and the gods for guidance whenever you can.

And that really is the best advice I can give. Living your path will often require you to trust in the energies that make it up. The current can carry you alone, or, for a time, may guide you into close proximity with other seekers on the same dark river. Groups may then form, although you should consider the river analogy further: How long can such freely floating Witches remain together?

Working with a Collective Will

Some of you may find what I'm about to say to be controversial. Let me apologize up front for that, but I have to say it anyway:

Covens, by their very nature, may not be able to last forever.

Now, I'm not talking about huge organizations of Pagans with possibly hundreds of members grouped up in local satellite circles and enclaves. Such groups actively recruit new members and act as useful sources for support and seasonal celebrations, becoming almost like official Churches or Temples of Paganism. By their emphasis on eclecticism and frequent recruiting, they provide a form of Wicca for the masses—useful for a lot of Pagans.

A true coven, however, is a tight group, usually consisting of thirteen or fewer members. All these Witches share a common set of beliefs and favored Gods and Goddesses. Ultimately, the members are all following the same current. But remember, they're freely floating bodies of a sort. Some might provide more resistance than others to the current. And while you can all hold hands in a circle, you can't hold hands throughout your nightly life. What happens to a member Witch in those solitary hours is often out of the control of a coven. Someone occasionally falls behind or surges forward in development. And if this happens to enough members. . . .

Should you wish to start a coven, keep in mind its potentially short lifespan. Rare is the group that stays together for decades—the group that is able to one day welcome and initiate the members' children. More likely is the group that recognizes its members' immediate and short-term needs, and helps these to be fulfilled.

Do you need a support group for your initial months as a dark Pagan? Is there a particular magickal goal that you need to work on with the help of others? Do you want others with whom to celebrate the nights of power? Even this last example is often a temporary reason for being in a coven, as over time the Sabbats may begin to take on different meanings to each member.

Let's not forget that Nocturnal Witchcraft is theurgic. The night provides inspiration and guidance for a reason: to help bring you closer to divinity in a form to which you can relate. Witchcraft of all types is very much about your personal relationship with the God and Goddess. The need to belong to or connect with something greater in the universe can always be fulfilled by that. But for the short-term, or for as long as it can survive, a coven can help provide something more.

If you do wish to align yourself with other Nocturnal Witches, make certain they are as much like you as possible. It won't be much help to you to join an existing coven that only slightly recognizes the dark through an occasional reference to a particular deity you're familiar with. Avoid the frustration of being the black Witch, so to speak, in such a family!

You'll likely need to form, not join, a coven. To my knowledge there are few active groups of dark Pagans, though they are out there (particularly in big cities). If you come across one of these preexisting covens, spend some time getting to know its members, as they'll undoubtedly be trying to better understand you. If they call themselves Witches or Pagans in this age, chances are they are what they claim to be. Long gone are the days when the word "witch" was used to describe those on the left-hand path. Still, through casual conversation you should be able to figure out if this group worships deity in the same way you do.

The first question you should ask when approaching an existing coven is: What makes your group dark? Too painfully obvious a question? Not at all. A dark coven should not just consist of people who like to wear black. Its members should be nightkind, in whatever way you consider yourself to be dark. Feel free to discuss with members some of the philosophies that intrigue you. Even if you haven't read the same books, you should still share some similar ideas and resonate with them if you are magickally compatible.

Conversation and some social time with Witches is the safest, easiest way to figure out if you're all a mystical fit. That's why, at first, joining or forming a coven are somewhat similar experiences. Both require getting to know a lot of Witches in a short period of time. When joining a coven, however, you are very much on the outside looking in. The group's philosophy and reason for being is usually firm, and you have to decide if you can be a part of this collective will. When forming a coven, you have to help identify what the collective will shall be, and then impose it on yourself and your willing group.

That's the key to forming or joining a coven: being able to work within a collective will.

Organization has a negative connotation in the minds of many who seek alternative spirituality. One of the first reasons we might have started looking elsewhere from, say, the Church, is because it suffers from being organized like, well, the Church. Organized religion, to me, has always seemed oppressive and not very willing to explore spirituality honestly. Groups like the Catholic and Orthodox Churches believe that to survive they need to maintain staunch control of their theology, and at times overzealously enforce their edicts. They fail to realize that it would be better for these and other Churches to fade away and be renewed every few decades than to cling to outmoded philosophies and "laws."

Covens, with their smaller, more focused scope, do not suffer from such problems. If their members start to feel enough dissonance, the coven naturally disbands. Never are irrelevant relationships maintained —rarely does one outgrow a coven and remain a member. Young Witches go on to become priests and priestesses in other covens. High Priests and Priestesses go on to pass on what they know to new young members, figuratively or literally.

Forming and Maintaining Nocturnal Covens

Again, to truly follow the Nocturnal current, chances are you will have to form your own coven. As mentioned previously, that will involve talking to a lot of Witches. Networking has never been easier than in this wired age, fortunately. Long gone is the need to purchase classified ads seeking Witches and to wait for these ads to appear in print. Now you can find relevant sites on the Internet, where Pagans with similar interests and who live close by are likely to spend time on bulletin boards. Couple some posts left at a few carefully chosen websites with some word of mouth buzz at a local occult bookstore and you're likely to draw more Witches than you'd ever be able to work with.

But what then? You have to make sure you're ready to handle the influx. The easiest way to do this is to be honest with yourself and these other Witches about what it is you're trying to accomplish. And be humble when approaching this goal.

You can be confident that the night is guiding you to create the right kind of group for you, especially if you ask the gods of night for help (highly recommended!). But don't come across to others as being so confident, if you know what I mean. Don't make potential coveners feel that you are presenting yourself as a Grand Master or Mistress of Darkness who needs followers. I won't insult you with an accusation that you would even try such a thing on purpose. No true Witch would consciously seek such power over others. I'm only reminding you of how easy it is to be perceived as power-hungry. After all, we who practice the magickal arts do desire power of a sort, but should never do so at the expense of others.

To succeed, you should be presenting to potential coveners a concise description of your vision. What is, or will be, your group's reason for being? We went over some examples in the last section, but you may have goals other than celebrating seasons or developing abilities in the early days of your Witchy life. Is there a particular goal you're working for? Only you know what your reasons for forming a coven are; have these reasons carefully laid out so that your potential coveners can know, too.

When forming a coven, make it known, up front, that it will be a democracy, and then do everything you can to make sure that this ideal is maintained. No one wants to be ruled over. Unless you've been a Witch for a long time and are working with a bunch of young ones who want to learn what you know, consider your coven to be an equal partnership. It is power struggles that destroy many covens, whether such groups are newly formed or a few years old.

It is a good idea to have a coven vote for a High Priest and/or a High Priestess. The person should be chosen based on his or her experience and willingness to devote time and energy to taking the lead on rituals. Also, he or she may be responsible for deciding how to distribute the roles of a rite (you'll find that more rituals are written for solitaries now than for covens, my books included). The role of High Priest or Priestess should not be an absolute right, however. Make it a tradition to have a new election every, say, Halloween.

With your organizational structure and purpose for being decided, you will have to then come up with a way to ensure your coven fulfills its purpose. No group will work well together if it rarely meets. Your coven will need to be able to practice group energy-raising on a regular basis, and you must also practice feeling comfortable with each other. Meeting on every Dark and Full Moon and every Sabbat might be difficult. Meeting on every Sabbat and a good number of planned alternating Dark and Full Moons is an excellent idea.

Before a celebration of one of these nights of power, the group should discuss any important short- and long-term magickal goals of its members. It may be relevant to work on some of them after the celebration part of the night's working; for instance, a banishing of a problem on a Dark Moon. If a covener feels he or she has a particularly strong need that may require extra preparation, this Witch should contact other members before a meeting night.

This book will not give rites for covens. The most important thing a magickal group has to learn is how to modify rites so that every member has a part. Even those who just joined a group should be able to feel as if they added to every rite they're in. If your coven can expand simple rites and work them as well as a solitary can work with himself or herself, then your group is a viable one. Remember, a coven has to have collective will.

You can try adapting simple rites for the nights of the Dark and Full Moons for group use, and should modify them further or rewrite such rites to suit everyone's feelings about the energies at work each night. The same applies to the simple Sabbat celebrations you'll be reading in the next chapter. Use them as starting points. Covens should modify them together, and both covens and solitaries should rethink them yearly. How you celebrate Halloween this year might not be relevant to your mindset next year. For a serious example, you may have lost a loved one and have more of a need to be reminded of his or her existence in the afterlife than of just celebrating what the night means.

To keep a coven running smoothly, it is important to have the group spend a little non-magickal time together after an evening's rite, too. I've always found that such socializing time does wonders for fostering the trust and good vibes necessary for successful group workings.

After your group has been together for a while and you become comfortable with its unique energies, come up with a name for the coven. Vote on it together, and have it somehow represent your group's ultimate aims. Feel free to write or e-mail me with details. I'd love to meet you and your dark group when I travel for booksignings, lectures, or even musical performances.

The Imminent End?

I don't want to sound like a doomsayer, but please do keep in mind that covens, nocturnal or otherwise, are not going to be eternally rewarding. You need to watch for signs that yours is possibly outliving its usefulness.

When meetings begin to feel like a burden on coveners, this is an early warning sign that things are coming apart. If you ever find yourself dreading such a gathering, you know you're in the wrong coven.

Other warnings: Is someone feeling held back? Or, conversely, is someone feeling frustratingly left out of a group's advancement? Some of these problems might result in one member leaving freely or after being asked to—frequent strife might indicate that a group has outlived its usefulness and its members are best off disbanding.

Let the night and the gods be your guides. Remember, Nocturnal Witchcraft should only be practiced by those drawn to the night, and a Nocturnal Coven should only add to the allure you feel for your religion. Only participate in such a group as long as this is the case.

Chapter Three

The Nocturnal Sabbats

Celebrating the Wheel of the Year is how a Witch strengthens his or her link with the magickal currents that flow through our world. As you may have gathered when encountering countless Sabbat descriptions and rites in the past, there is no true or proper way to do such connecting.

What you're about to read just happen to be my preferred methods for connecting with the energies of the Sabbats now. You can feel free to take some inspiration from these rites and change them to suit your own needs, or work with them for a while as they are.

Just *do* connect with these nights of power in some form—you'll be glad you did.

Power at the Core

Considering that the Wheel of the Year begins with Halloween, we'll begin here with the celebration of that Sabbat, and follow with rites

25

honoring Yule, Candlemas, Ostara, Beltane, Midsummer's Eve, Lammas, and Mabon. Each celebration rite will be preceded by a short look at the energies at play during each night, as well as any preparations you'll need to make for a particular rite.

You will find that these celebrations take advantage of the energies or thoughtforms that have been built up around the Sabbats over centuries. Put simply, even if there never were energies associated with these nights granted by some universal tribunal, the years of association we humans have granted the dates gives them significance, and power.

Thoughtforms bring this real power to each Sabbat, making these nights more than just set-aside, random dates. In some ways, our ancestors have made these nights into the batteries that they are—we can now tap into this energy to enhance our attunement with our nocturnal nature.

As you'll soon see, you'll be literally drawing some of the energies of these built-up thoughtforms into yourself.

The seasonal dates of Sabbats can only apply to one hemisphere. In this book, and in my practice, I go with the Northern Hemisphere, as that's where I live. If you're below the equator, so to speak, you can swap the dates with their opposites. For instance, Yule can be celebrated on your, not our, Winter Solstice. However, you may still find it best to celebrate the days on their northern equivalents, as these are the days that the majority of ancient cultures built up thoughtforms around. That is, if you break down the Wheel of the Year by world cultures that celebrated each day, you'll find that more Northern Hemisphere cultures honored them. Making an argument for swapping the days, however, is that in the south the dark months begin with the northern spring, not Autumnal Equinox. North or south dates—it's a choice you'll have to make with built-up power kept in mind.

Halloween

On this powerful night the harvest season comes to an end, making Halloween (October 31) both the end of the Wheel of the Year and its beginning. But it is no New Year celebration that gives Halloween its power. Built up around this night is a thoughtform that amplifies the idea that as the seasons and crops go through cycles and thereby return, we too shall live on after our own deaths. After possibly thousands of years of such association, humans have built up a very real link between Halloween and the delicate balance of life and death. Coupled with the recognition of the ancient myth of the Dying God, who is said to pass on this night, it is a religious night of unparalleled power—arguably more tangible power than that of any other Sabbat.

Tangible, that is, because you can see the unseen on this night.

It is due to the mental associations we've built around Halloween that it is said to be the time when the veil between the worlds is at its thinnest. The celebration you are about to read takes into account this energy, providing time for experimentation with divination or necromancy.

It is fitting that this most powerful of Sabbats is the one that fully ushers in the dark months. While the very day after Mabon or the Autumnal Equinox brings with it more darkness than light, Halloween is the first Sabbat that is appreciably enveloped in night. And even longer nights are yet to come.

Remember, most Nocturnal Witchcraft techniques and rites work better after sunset, making the dark half of the year most important for nightkind, to say the least. The dark half of the year is when you'll have the most opportunities to connect with the night. Halloween's power only drives this into your subconscious. If seeing is believing, you'll believe in the power of all nights after experiencing this unique one.

To celebrate this rite you'll need a fully set-up altar, with a notable difference: The drink and treat that you normally leave outside the circle will now be placed on the altar (you'll find this in the other Sabbat rites, too).

Also, you'll need to pick a Halloween symbol to put between the food and drink. This can be a tiny jack o' lantern or even a toy skeleton (but not the skull you used in your initiation—that should have been buried). Ideally the Halloween symbol will represent the energies of death and rebirth to you, but even something festive can work because of Halloween's numerous cartoon-like associations with the macabre. This symbol, as with the ones you'll be gathering for the other Sabbats, can be used once, or every year. As you'll see, it will house the thought-form of the season during your celebration.

Make sure the symbol is making physical contact with your drink and treat. All three should be as far in front of your nocturnal portal or skrying device as the space on your altar top allows.

Finally, choose a deity that you feel represents the holiday to you. When doing a powerful, true invocation—when you strive to wear the skin of the deity or assume its godform—you can only call one deity. However, if you plan on doing simple invocation, you can call both a God and Goddess. If working with others, too, then it's possible for one person to call a God and another a Goddess. Keep this in mind for all of the Sabbats.

In these rites, we will not be reenacting a myth cycle. Don't feel obligated to choose a deity that is connected by lore to the date. For instance, you don't need to pick a Dying God for this rite, but can choose one of the Gods or Goddesses associated with the Underworld.

You will need to write an invocation to your deity of choice expressing your desire for his or her company on this night of power. Also, you may want to ask for his or her help in contacting the dead. This rite is written with a step that enables you to try some kind of afterlife communication experiment. This can be a form of mini-séance, the use of a Ouija board, or a formal necromantic rite that you find in some book (if you're a regular reader of mine, you already have a couple of such rites). You can even modify the Inanna Rite given in the last chapter of this grimoire, although it is possibly too elaborate to easily incorporate into a Sabbat celebration. It's your choice as to how you try to actually experience the power of this night. Have on hand the items those rituals require, including an item relating to the deceased (if you wish to speak to someone in particular and not just to any loved one who might have a message for you).

Try to have a God or Goddess representation on your altar that matches the deity most appropriate to your working, if you can. However, a statue of the deity should *not* be the Sabbat symbol placed between your drink and treat.

Try to perform the rite as close to midnight as you can arrange, but begin before midnight if possible.

The Halloween Rite

Cast a circle, without invoking deity.

Skry your nocturnal portal while saying:

> *And so, the dark ether begins to have full sway.*
> *Increasingly difficult to quell, the power of night lingers each weakening day.*
> *Yet on this eve does the fabric of darkness ripple and tear.*
> *It is this sundered veil of ether that passes over us now.*
> *The worlds surrounding us are no longer those of seen and unseen.*
> *On this night, it is the realms of the living and dead we stand between.*

Wait and see if any symbols appear to you, but do not worry too much about interpreting them now. There will be plenty of time for that later.

At this point you should attempt your preferred method for contacting the other side. If there are steps in the rite that thank the deity for being with you, however, save performing those until the end of the Halloween Rite, maintaining your link with Divine a bit longer (for the coming steps that involve the Halloween symbol).

And you do need a link. If you do not wish to perform a necromantic rite, invoke a God or Goddess of your choice at this time.

After you either contact the afterlife or just call to a deity, turn your attention to the Halloween symbol you selected. Pick it up with two hands and rest it in your palms. Lift your arms up just high enough so you have to tilt your head back a few degrees to see the symbol above you. Make certain you can still see where you are going, for you are now about to begin walking.

Walk clockwise around your altar, visualizing that you are moving through ribbons of varying shades of darkness. That is, imagine that you are walking through the sundered veil of night, allowing the Halloween symbol to pass through these pockets of energy and dark potential. Feel the symbol pulsing with the exposure.

Go to the west quarter of your circle, facing west (with your back to the altar). Lower the symbol to chest level, and bring it close to you. Gaze off into the darkness of the west and say:

Farewell, Lord, as you recede into the darkness.
I, your child, shall be searching for your essence in each growing shadow,
and will welcome your return on the darkest night of the year.

Close your eyes and feel the symbol pulsing in your hands.

Rotate clockwise to face the altar; walk toward it. Return the symbol to its place touching the drink and treat.

If it has such a step, perform the part from the necromantic rite that lets the link to divinity recede. If you did your own invocation, thank the God or Goddess for lending energy to your celebration.

Close your circle.

Enjoy the specially charged drink and treat.

Place the Halloween symbol somewhere (but not on your altar) where no one else will touch it. Take a look at or hold this symbol over the coming year whenever you need to feel a connection with the energies of this night—whenever you wish to meditate on or work magick pertaining to the forces of life and death.

Yule

As interesting and ironic as it may be, while everyone else in the Northern Hemisphere is celebrating the coming of new light to the world—the start of the solar year around December 20—nightkind can relish the longest night of the year! Yule or the Winter Solstice is also a good time for dark ones to recognize that our seasons are governed by the sun, even if we prefer to work by its light reflected off the moon. But the greatest power in this night lies in the extra dark hours with which we can sympathetically attune.

Yule marks the mythical rebirth of the Dying God. As such, it is also a great night to be reborn, in a figurative way. We can perform rituals to change our lives, or just renew and reinforce our goals. All around you the holiday season will be in full force, complete with ancient Pagan and Druidic symbolism such as decorated trees. The good will that many people are spreading, when not stressing out over crowded mall parking lots and long lines, does translate into a tangible vibe you may pick up nightly approaching Yule. It's another seasonal thought-form that you can tap into, and one that will help you make positive changes to the world around you.

And again, it's the longest night of the year!

As with all of the Sabbat celebrations, you'll have to select the appropriate deity to work with. For the Yule rite, you can do anything from invoke a universal aspect of the God to pick a particular one having to do with rebirth, such as Khepera. Interestingly, this beetle-headed Egyptian God has both solar and nocturnal aspects, making him a good, if not traditional, deity to call on this night of the solar Wheel's rebirth.

Whichever God or even Goddess you pick, be sure to write an invocation that involves a request for help with your rite. If you plan on trying to do some magick for change in your life, bring up these goals in the invocation. Tonight is the night to be reborn in some magickal way, or even to begin a new phase of your more mundane goals. If you are only celebrating the holiday, ask the deity to make you aware of the energies around you and let these energies act on their own, as energies can, possibly for your benefit.

Finding a Yule symbol for this rite should be simple. Mistletoe or a generic tree decoration are good choices. Just pick something that reminds you of the season—don't worry about whether or not it has anything to do with the solstice itself. The symbols are only aids to tapping into a particular thoughtform. This symbol, as with all Sabbat ones, should be placed on your altar touching the drink and treat. Put them as far before the nocturnal portal as space allows.

To clarify, the reason that the drink and treat are always on the altar for Sabbats and always outside the circle for other nocturnal workings has to do with which energies you want to take into yourself. During a Sabbat you want the energy of the thoughtform, hence the contact with the symbol. For other nocturnal rites you want the energy of night's ether, which swirls about your circle.

You'll also need one red candle. Wrap it in black cloth and leave it on the floor, just inside your circle at the west quarter. If the candle is a taper, have an extra holder for it on your altar (where the candle will ultimately end up during the rite). Try to burn pine incense or actual tree needles, if you can.

The Yule Rite

Cast a circle.

Skry the portal while saying:

> *On this night, the dark ether resonates with new reflected light.*
> *Yet it is the darkness that has full sway.*
> *On this night, the dark ether returns to us a rejuvenated link to Divine.*
> *May our lives be so rejuvenated.*

Allow any symbols to appear in the portal, but don't worry about interpreting them just yet.

Invoke the deity of your choice.

Perform any magick that you have selected for this night (again, a spell designed to bring about some new stage in your life).

Look out into the darkness to the east. Try to imagine a subtle glow to the ether—sort of what you see in the portal when it is properly lighted for skrying.

Slowly turn in place, observing this visualized glow in the darkness that surrounds your circle. By the time you complete your rotation to once again face the east, the circle around you should feel somewhat warmer. The dark ether seems almost orange now, no? Almost the color you see behind your eyelids when closing them against a bright light?

Without taking your eyes off the ether's glow, feel for the symbol on your altar and pick it up with your receiving hand (again, the one you don't write with). Do not look at the symbol yet.

Walk clockwise around your altar to the east. Extend your receiving arm and see the symbol surrounded by the glowing ether. Touch the perimeter of the circle with the symbol.

Move clockwise, keeping the symbol in contact with the circle perimeter. Feel the glowing ether charging the object.

Stop when you reach the west and kneel on the floor, but do not break contact between the circle and symbol. Use your other, or projecting, hand to pick up the wrapped candle. Say:

> *And from the gates of the west does the God return.*
> *For rising in the east, the sun's light is most fully reflected*
> *by whatever lurks in the dark of the west.*
> *In rising from the west, the dead escape the setting sun to enter nocturnal life.*

Stand, and with your receiving hand continue to draw energy into the Yule symbol as you move clockwise to the east. Keep your projecting hand and candle at your side.

After you complete the circumambulation, return clockwise to your spot before the altar. Place the symbol again between the drink and treat.

Unwrap the red candle and light it from the right altar candle, which is next to your God symbol or statue. Stand the red candle up in front of the right altar candle.

Thank the deity of your choice for aiding you on this night of power.

Close the circle.

Enjoy the specially charged drink and treat.

Keep the Yule symbol somewhere where no one else will touch it, and hold it whenever you feel a need to connect with the energies of this longest night. Allow the red candle to burn away completely, and enjoy the prevalent darkness.

Candlemas

On February 2, halfway through winter, Candlemas (also called Imbolc) reminds us that it won't always be this cold—gradual warming is approaching. With that warming will also come the months of light, and this is the last Sabbat in the Wheel where night is dominant. Of course, nightkind do not turn to dust with sunlight and we have no reason to be saddened by the coming loss of prevailing hours of nocturnal time. Instead, we should remember that this night is one of future promise. We are reminded that as a new spring is approaching, so too does another eventual dark cycle . . . and many other new things in our lives in between.

Candlemas is a perfect night to begin something new. It is a night of hidden potential, after all. The thoughtform attributed with it is one of reawakening fire and vitality, so you can plan a spell that will help you with some future goal that seems far from coming to fruition without the help of a little bit of magick. Gather any materials you need for this spell.

Whether you do any magick this night, though, you will need a symbol for the Sabbat celebration. Anything that has a dormant potential within it can be used. Choices for the nature-minded include a bag of seeds that need to bloom in the spring or a winter twig. Witches who are more urban can use a black or silver lighter they bought for this purpose, as no artificial device captures the essence of hidden fire better. Whatever symbol you choose, place it between the drink and treat on the altar.

While the Goddess Brigid is most often associated with this Sabbat, you can choose to invoke any nocturnal deity with whom you feel most comfortable asking for long-term help. Calling one of the deities of Night Personified makes the most sense, as Candlemas is still a time of predominant darkness. Further, whatever long-term goal for which you do magick will be developing as a thoughtform in the black ether over the next several months, and the Gods of Night Personified will be guiding it along without any dependency on, say, the moon's phase.

If you are performing magick on Candlemas, write your invocation to reflect this. Otherwise, phrase your call to ask the deity to be with you as you seek to maintain a link to the receding darkness around you.

The Candlemas Rite

Cast a circle.

Skry the nocturnal portal as you say:

No bonfires blaze in this chamber, yet the hidden fires burn in the darkness about.
The hard ground's icy blades shine with moonlight full of promise;

any snow will reflect even brighter silver.
May the decreasing hours of darkness bring increased potency
to the nocturnal workings they will contain.

Allow any symbols to appear to you for later interpretation.

Invoke your chosen deity.

Perform any magick you have prepared.

Using your receiving hand, pick up the symbol from the altar and carry it to the east, moving clockwise.

Facing east, kneel and touch the object to the ground, just inside the perimeter of your circle. Do not make contact with the circle, though, and do not let go of the symbol.

Even if it means imagining you are looking through numerous walls, visualize that about a hundred yards away there is an orange disc the size of your circle. It is creeping along the ground toward you, as if it were a spotlight projected into the darkness from a moving helicopter above.

Say:

New life approaches the barren lands.

Continue to visualize the approaching disc. When it is only a few feet away from your circle, imagine that the disc is slowing. Say:

Yet even in the darkness of Candlemas does the promise lurk.
May all the coming nights be so filled with promise.

Imagine the orange disc coming into contact with your circle. Try to see the silver perimeter of your circle change into orange for a few seconds (note that the circle in the Nocturnal Tradition is cast with silver light). When you see this change, drag the Candlemas symbol you hold in your receiving hand across the ground to make brief contact with the circle's perimeter. Feel the electric tingle pulsing in your receiving hand.

Dramatically pull the symbol away, visualizing that the orange sphere is gone and that the magick circle is once again silver.

Move clockwise around the circle to return to your place before the altar. Replace the charged symbol between the drink and treat.

Thank the deity for being with you.

Close the circle.

Take part in the drink and treat.

Store the Candlemas symbol someplace safe. Pick it up when you need to be reminded of either the spell you did or the fact that any night can contain magickal promise.

Ostara

The threshold of the light months is marked by the Spring Equinox, or Ostara (around March 21). Until Mabon comes in September, this is our last chance to work with at least twelve hours of night. Yet as the light energies begin to take over, we can adjust our schedules to take advantage of the fewer dark hours. With such awareness, the night hours will only be more rewarding in their potency. For a few months, we will need to be extra careful about finding time to plant magickal seeds within the shortening nights available to us.

Speaking of planting seeds, the springtime energies being released on this night make Ostara a perfect time to work magick related to fertility, be it sexual or financial. As the earth recovers from barren winter, we honor the dying Goddess' return that makes it possible. In cultures such as Sumer (Inanna) and Greece (Demeter), the return of the dying Goddesses brought new life and joy. You can choose an Underworld deity to invoke this night, or one that represents the Full Moon.

Why the Full Moon? To enhance the fertile power of the Sabbat, you should perform the celebration on the night itself, but plan any magick you do to be a two-part ritual. Begin a working during the Sabbat celebration, and finish it on the night of the next Full Moon. For instance, a candle used in a spell can be snuffed (not blown out) and then magickally recharged and relit on the Full Moon. Keep this scheduling in mind when writing your invocation; let the words reflect how many nights separate Ostara from the Full Moon, for instance, as well as your plan to act again on the coming night.

For this rite you have to use a specific symbol for Ostara: a colored egg. Besides being a symbol that was always associated with this night, it is one that will serve a specific purpose in the celebration. You can either paint a real egg yourself (black and silver are okay, or you can choose any colors you wish), or obtain a plastic one. If you do use a real egg, make sure it is hardboiled, and store it with care after the rite! For the celebration, balance it between the drink and treat on your altar.

The Ostara Rite

Cast a circle.

Skry the portal while saying:

> *Once again the night prepares to recede—*
> *prepares to give sway to the daylight hours,*
> *to give the sun its chance to reawaken the seasonal sleepers of nature.*
> *And so we prepare to maximize our use of the decreasing quiet,*
> *to craft even more of our magicks while the nightly sleepers rest.*

Wait a few moments to allow any images to appear in the portal; you can interpret them later.

Invoke the deity you chose.

Perform any magick you planned for this night. If you do a spell, end it by visualizing the Full Moon within your nocturnal portal. Hold the image for about ten seconds, planting in your mind the coming manifestation of the spell's goal.

Look down at the Ostara egg. Imagine that you are adjusting your vision to perceive the object's spiritual core. See it? It is a glowing orange sphere within, and is about the size of a yolk.

When you're certain you can imagine the glowing core, immediately look away and move clockwise to the eastern quarter of your circle. Do not stop at this quarter, however. Begin, instead, to walk the perimeter of the circle at a brisk pace. Your eyes should be focused on the ground where the silver, glowing perimeter line of your circle bisects the thick blackness outside and the lighter, candlelit darkness inside. Move quickly around the circle, but keep a sense of your position.

Every time you pass the west quarter, quickly glance away from the circle's perimeter to see the egg on the altar. Note how the core is growing larger and brighter with each circumambulation you make. Take note of the size of the core and return your gaze to the black/silver/lighter black path you're following.

After a couple of times around the west quarter, you'll notice that the growing orange core will begin to swallow the egg and even the altar. When the sphere has reached this approximate three-foot diameter, begin to speed up your circumambulations.

The goal is to fill the magick circle with the egg's core—to eventually see the orange glow in your field of vision as you're staring down at the perimeter of the circle. Perhaps after thirteen times around the circle, you will be seeing black/silver/orange and feeling the heat in the circle. When this happens, continue around the circle to end up at the west quarter.

Quickly kneel without turning (that is, with your left shoulder to the west), and deliberately place your open palms on the ground. Imagine that you are pushing the orange sphere into the earth. Your left hand should stay just within the silver circle's perimeter, and both hands should feel a rush from the act of pushing the circle's raised energy down. Make sure to see in your mind's eye the sphere moving down.

Remain in this position until you feel and see that the entire orange sphere you built up has disappeared into the ground. After the circle feels once again normal, stand and turn clockwise to face the altar.

Look at the egg and note that there still is a glowing orange core within it. Say:

> *The egg retains a link to the energy—*
> *to the symbolic sacrifice I made to earth this night.*
> *As new life abounds and the night sacrifices its dominance,*
> *may I retain the same link to hidden potential.*

Take a few steps to your normal position before the altar and extend your receiving hand, palm down, over the egg. Feel the energy there.

Thank the deity for being with you.

Close the circle.

Enjoy the drink and treat that are infused with the energy of life.

The egg should be on the altar again for your next Full Moon rite to lend its energies to the recharging of the spell you did this night. After that time, it should only be handled when you need a boost from this night's fertile energies.

Beltane

When the sun sets April 30, another fertility feast begins. Beltane heralds in the second half of the Wheel, which began with Halloween. Celebrations for this Sabbat have included dancing around bonfires and a Maypole, in a sense invoking the energies of spring that are abundant. Sex magick and fertility rites work well on this night, too.

Myth cycles recognize that the Goddess is pregnant with the God by this point, and so does the following dark rite. Also, the celebration helps you consider new things the second half of the year may hold for you. Beltane is the first Sabbat where the day is longer than the night, and is a time to rethink how we will spend the rest of the lighter months. You should have already begun adapting to new hours of activity, finding your own schedule to make more productive use of the magickal hours of night that are still available. But if not, now is a good time to make such adjustments.

The best symbol to use for Beltane is a phallic one. No need to build a Maypole, though. You can use anything elongated that triggers thoughts of fertility in your mind, either due to its natural attributes or a modification you make to it. For example, a pinecone works well as a natural symbol. In the case of adding something to a symbol, consider painting a wooden dowel black with a spiral silver stripe wrapping around it from end to end. Feel free to get creative here, especially if you're performing a sex magick rite such as the one in Part Five.

Whatever symbol you choose, make sure it is standing up between your drink and treat. This will be easier to accomplish with a pinecone than with a dowel, which will require some kind of base.

On your altar you'll also need whatever items your particular spell requires. As with the other celebrations, write your invocation to reflect the Sabbat and the magick you hope to accomplish. You may wish to pick a deity associated with fertility, even a Full Moon one.

The Beltane Rite

Cast a circle.

Skry the nocturnal portal as you say:

What was set in motion on Ostara has come to fruition.
Our nights are becoming shorter, yet growing in potency and becoming more precious.
On this night, we seek to attune with the energies that lurk within the Dark Mother.
The energies preparing her for bringing forth divine life.

Spend a few moments allowing any symbols to appear to you for later interpretation.

Invoke your chosen deity.

Perform any magick you have prepared.

Standing before your altar, stare down at the Beltane symbol. Spend a few moments imagining that you can see at the symbol's base a glowing, silver sphere.

Reach out with your receiving hand and extend your pointer finger. Touch the outer edge of the glowing sphere. Feel a little bit of the energy rush up your arm.

Move your hand back a few inches and note how the energy follows it, forming a silver ribbon.

With your connection established, begin to walk around the left side of your altar, pulling the silver ribbon of light with you. Try to be comfortable for the circumambulations you make. If you're right handed, hold your left receiving hand against your chest with your pointer finger always pointing toward the symbol. If you're left handed, extend slightly your right receiving hand and finger.

Pull the etheric silver ribbon around the symbol. Imagine that each time you complete a circumambulation you are adding a wide layer of glowing light, perhaps three inches tall. Each trip around the circle should result in a higher rod of etheric energy. You can imagine the ribbon getting wider as you progress, but try to see it as being at most six inches wide.

Try to increase your speed a little with each circumambulation, too.

Continue building the column even after you've made a glowing rod that's taller than the physical one on the altar. Your goal is to send the growing column right up into contact with the overhead edge of your magickal circle/sphere. Remember, when casting a circle, you are really creating a sphere of sacred space. The circle you cast on the ground really creates one dome over, one dome under you. Your goal now is to connect the silver column to that sphere's "ceiling."

Once you've finished raising the column of light, feel the ribbon pull into the column and away from your receiving finger. After this happens, make your final circumambulation, and make certain it's the fastest, most enthusiastic one—a peak of sorts. Spiral in to your spot before the altar during this last almost run around the circle.

Stop before the altar and use your momentum to swing both arms around in front of you. Seemingly grab the two sides of the pulsing column. Feel the energy of your circumambulation fire up the column as your hands stop perhaps eight inches apart. You've just made an energy offering. The dark ether will return this energy to you many times over during the coming nights.

Imagine that the column is starting to dissipate. Reinforce your act by saying:

Potent nights approach.

Thank the deity for being with you.

Close the circle.

Take part in the drink and treat.

Store the Beltane symbol someplace safe. Take it out when you need to be reminded of either the magick you did or the potency of each short night this coming summer.

Midsummer's Eve

Oddly named when you think about it, Midsummer's Eve (around June 21) is the first night of summer. It's actually the "mid-light-months' eve," and is the shortest night of the year. This solstice is an excellent night to remain awake until sunrise, if you can arrange your schedule to accommodate. Try giving yourself this sort of nocturnal energy boost to get through the rest of the light months, if only for a symbolic reaffirmation of your chosen dark path. You may need such a boost to remind yourself of night's wonders, too, as on this date of solar power there is less dark ether to work with.

As with Halloween, Midsummer's Eve has built around it a thought-form that associates the night with the veil between the worlds being thin. People who worked outdoors and traditionally tried to take advantage of as much daylight as possible would have had too little sleep on this solstice. Did they have mild hallucinations as a result? Whatever caused them to come about, associations between this night and the invisible world abound—again, a thoughtform built up for Sabbat celebrants to take advantage of and attune with.

This is another great night to perform a necromantic rite of your choice. Doing so may even help you choose which deity to invoke. If you plan no magick, related to the other side or this one, try to invoke a deity that is associated with either the Underworld or the myths of Descent and Rebirth. Growing darkness is reborn on this night.

In addition to the materials required for your magick or spell, you will need a Midsummer's Eve symbol. For our purposes, though, it won't be one associated with summer and sunlight. The best thing to use is a bit of graveyard soil, if you can get it. Morbid as it seems, this symbol will directly tap into the types of folklore associated with this night in "Old Europe." You'll be partly reenacting one of these legends in this rite. If graveyard "dust," as it's called, is unavailable, try to get some soil from a decrepit, abandoned building or some patch of land that has been left to decay. Whatever soil you do get, rest it on a flat stone on the altar, between the drink and treat.

The Midsummer's Eve Rite

Cast a circle.

Skry the portal, saying:

Night's potency cannot be contained in the few hours allowed it this dominating day.
The mysteries of dream, of the unseen, seep into the world of the waking.
On the brink of darkness's return, the veil lifts again.

Allow any images to appear in the portal; you can interpret them later.

Invoke the deity you chose.

Perform any magick—preferably necromantic—that you planned for this night.

Move around the left side of your altar and go to the east edge of your circle. Look out into the darkness and say:

Night's potency: pure treasure pockets of energy awaiting discovery.

Imagine that a few feet away from your circle is a glowing purple sphere, half coming out of the ground. Begin a circumambulation.

As you move to the south, note that there are two or three more of these spheres to the southeast. Continue this first circumambulation, noting spheres here and there outside your circle.

When you return to the east, you should begin to notice twice as many spheres outside your sacred space. Continue your second circumambulation, moving faster now, and noting how many more half-buried purple globes there actually are.

Do another circumambulation, moving even faster. Realize on this third time around that the night is alive with these strange, purple spheres of energy, all half buried. All are energy batteries waiting to be tapped. Let the knowledge of all this available power, combined with the elation of this fastest circumambulation, fill you with a mystical high. You should feel this emotional energy rising.

Stop when you reach the east again, and pivot to look toward the altar. Breathe deeply, extend your projecting hand (the one you write with), and exhale. Imagine a purple beam firing toward the altar from your palm. It should seem to pass through the back side of your nocturnal portal and disappear.

Walk slowly, clockwise, to return to your place before the altar. Look down and see what you have done.

The soil is glowing, containing its own pocket of purple energy—the focused potency of a shortened night.

Thank the deity for being with you.

Close the circle.

Enjoy the drink and treat.

Find a special bag or pouch to pour the soil into, preferably a black one. It is a bag of night's potency and may aid you during any daytime mystical workings you are forced to do throughout the year. Just don't open it until next year, when you should pour out the contents and gather new soil to charge. If you'd like a Bag of Night that you can reach into for ritual purposes, check out Part Five.

Lammas

August 2 is traditionally the beginning of the harvest season, and Lammas is a night for us to reap what we've sown all year. We can do this in normal waking consciousness by following through on long-range projects and workings. Mystically, harvest season is an important time to see if our long-range rites are also working as we had hoped. It's a great time to look after your own magickal and material prosperity.

The Lammas rite recognizes this harvest thoughtform, as well as the fact that the nights are getting longer. We are approaching the dark months, though fall may still seem far away in the warm days of early August.

Gather materials for a prosperity spell of some sort—the kind of magick that will work best on this night. Choose a deity that you feel will be beneficial to such magick.

Also, find a Lammas symbol. This must be something that still has some life in it—something that is still green, if you will. Yet it must be something that will inevitably die. A fresh-cut flower is excellent, particularly the aromatic lily that reminds us of the season approaching. You can also use the branch of a small plant. Keep this temporarily living object in a small vase or cup of water for the rite, and position the drink and treat to touch the container.

The Lammas Rite
Cast a circle.

Skry the nocturnal portal as you say:

> *Cut and gathered, before the withering begins, is the bounty.*
> *May we harvest all we can from these potent hours of darkness.*
> *May we potently use the many hours of darkness approaching.*

Spend a few moments allowing any symbols to appear to you for later interpretation.

Invoke your chosen deity.

Perform any magick you have prepared.

Standing before your altar, spend a few moments observing the cup or vase holding the Lammas symbol. Imagine that it is glowing green. The entire container houses life-giving energy.

Try to now see the etheric double of the Lammas symbol. It is a glowing, silver version of the plant or flower that permeates the entire living thing. You should be able to imagine the entire stem, even the part disappearing into the cup or vase. See how the silver line of the stem is surrounded and nourished by the green, glowing water.

Now, imagine that the pointer finger on your receiving hand has, connected to it, a black sickle blade. This should seem blacker in your open-eyed visualization than does the candlelit darkness around you.

Gaze again at the Lammas symbol, and its merging of green and silver energy.

Spin around three times *counter*clockwise, catching a glimpse of the glowing symbol each time.

At the end of your last rotation, slash at the center of the cup or vase with your etheric sickle. See a disruption of the green and silver energy fields, and feel some of the energy of each of those fields rush up your sickle and into your receiving arm.

Quickly pull the plant or flower out of the vase with your projecting hand. Lay the symbol on the altar with its top or flower touching the treat and its stem base touching the cup holding the drink. Note how its silver glow is still there, yet fainter.

Allow the imagined sickle to dissipate. Then, lift with your receiving hand the cup or vase that is still glowing very green. Use the finger of your projecting hand to sprinkle a few drops of the glowing water on both your drink and treat. As you do so, say:

For our use, from the Gods, life's energy.

Return the cup to the altar.

Thank the deity for helping you this night.

Close the circle.

Take part in the specially charged drink and treat.

Hang the Lammas plant or flower somewhere out of reach to let it dry out. You can then store it someplace safe and pick it up whenever you need a quick infusion of energy.

Mabon

Finally the much-awaited equinox arrives. Mabon (around September 21) brings us equal night and day, this time with the promise of increasing darkness to follow. It's the peak harvest, and an excellent time to recharge anything you did on Lammas for prosperity. The thought-form built up around this night is similar to that of Lammas, yet with the bonus of extra hours of power available to nightkind.

You can choose a Dying God to invoke, or any other deity you feel comfortable working with for whatever spell you're planning. About the Dying God—we realize on this night that the mythical Dying God is preparing for his death, but there is nothing sad about this myth. Reflect upon the legend as a reminder of how new things will come from the dark months. Your nights are about to become a lot more magickal, and for this all nightkind should be thankful.

Mabon is a type of thanksgiving night, by the way, so you will want to gather a special "harvesty" drink and treat. This should be something that feels seasonal to you. Orange or so-called winter vegetables like squash and sweet potatoes are a good choice, if you like them. The drink can be something like cider. If possible, you may want to have a late harvest meal prepared before you do the rite. That way, when you complete your celebration you can carry the charged treat and drink to the table and have a mystical thanksgiving. Such a late-night Mabon feast can be wonderful, as long as you plan on staying up long enough to digest!

The Mabon symbol should be something that you can leave out for the next month and then some. That is, something that will remind you of the essence of fall and prepare you for Halloween. A little scarecrow or a cornucopia, perhaps? Maybe some drying colorful leaves or a coated piece of decorative corn? Pick something that reminds you of this magickal time of year, and something you'll want to have out in plain sight. For now, set it up between the special drink and treat.

The Mabon Rite

Cast a circle.

Skry the nocturnal portal as you say:

Preparing to descend into the Underworld, God views the deaths we cause.
These lives we take are ones we nourished, and in harvest we ensure we shall go on.

Allow any symbols to appear to you for later interpretation.

Invoke your chosen deity.

Perform any magick you have prepared.

Pick up the Mabon symbol with your receiving hand and look out into the darkness.

Try to see a faint, orange mist in the ether of night. Think of the mist as particles of solar energy that are trying to maintain cohesion with each other in the darkness. Say:

In mere moments, night's hours will prevail over those of day,
granting us new vitality as the barren months approach.
To make way, we now banish predominant day.

Moving around the right side of the altar, begin to walk around the circle counterclockwise. Do so with your head turned to the right, so that you can see the orange mist in the darkness. Also, hold the Mabon symbol at about chest level and a foot or so away. It should seem as if you are presenting it to the night.

Visualize on your first counterclockwise circumambulation that some of the orange particles are winking out of existence as they shine on the Mabon symbol.

Increasing speed on your second circumambulation, imagine that most of the particles are dying out, sending energy in the form of light to the Mabon symbol you hold.

Increase speed again on your third circumambulation, and imagine that any final particles you pass are disappearing as they send their energy into the circle and the Mabon symbol.

Return to your spot before the altar and stop dramatically. Quickly switch the symbol to your projecting hand and place it down between the treat and drink. Say:

> *We take for our use the life energies that abound.*
> *Can any thanks ever repay such plenty?*

Thank the deity for being with you.

Close the circle.

Enjoy your special drink and treat, or, if you're having a thanksgiving meal of sorts, carry the charged food and the Mabon symbol to the table and enjoy their energies there.

Keep the Mabon symbol out until Halloween, but try to keep it out of general reach or handling. You may want to use it as a table centerpiece occasionally over the coming weeks.

Part Two

Reading Thoughts, Divining the Future

Chapter Four

Grabbing Thoughts

In *Nocturnal Witchcraft* we explored how to dowse minds—how to essentially ask silent questions of another's mind and then figure out which of the possible responses is correct. Seemingly the stuff of fantasy, the technique works.

This chapter is designed to pick up where the other book left off, advancing the ability of mind dowsing to a more advanced form. Unlike the other chapters in this grimoire, this one contains techniques that might not work for those who try them based on standard occult knowledge, hence my warning in the introduction. However, you might be one of the exceptions. Check out what's contained in the next few pages. If you can get the techniques to work, great. If not, it's up to you to decide if you want to seek out and perform the preliminary rites and techniques upon which they're based.

Tell you what—I'll even toss in little refreshers throughout the chapter that might help you along, whether you've experimented with mind dowsing or not.

Mind dowsing is based on the concept of what I call the pull. It's a feeling you get when something is right. So, if you were to try to get someone thinking along a certain line of thought, and then dowsed his or her mind using possible answers, you could feel which answer is right. For example, tell someone to think of either heads or tails, visualize two coins in your mind—one for each side—and then feel which coin pulls you. Is it heads or tails? Your mind will tell you, with training.

Sensing the pull for the first time takes practice—again, with specific techniques. But if you've ever succeeded at dowsing for something with, say, a pendulum or Y rod, you might already have some experience you could apply. Think of your projecting hand (the one you write with) as the dowsing device and move over imaginary representations of possible answers looking for the pull. That's just about the best synopsis I can give here.

Now, how far can such dowsing go? Certainly, snatching an exact sentence from someone's mind would take a long time. To do so, you would possibly have to go through an imaginary alphabet of floating letters, dowsing one letter of a message at a time. This could take so long that your subject's mind would wander, and chances are he or she would physically do the same!

However, through the use of intuition, getting the gist of a thought might only take an instant. And the repeated use of mind dowsing will expand your intuition. This is a wonderful boost to a magickal lifestyle. As your intuition expands, you'll find that there is a lot of useful information out there, whether it's gleaned from thoughts or the guidance that night and the deities provide.

When working on the techniques here in Part Two, begin listening to your intuition, whether it is day or night. With increasing frequency, you'll begin to get feelings that a certain action or way to go is right. As long as you're not acting on dangerous impulses, do try the options suggested by these gut feelings first. You may be surprised to find you're nearly always led in the right direction.

Mind Dowsing, Evolved

The concept of dowsing thoughts as tangible items might seem strange at first, but after a little practice the pull in your projecting hand will become a very real feeling. And such a feeling only adds to your mind's acceptance of the entire process, thereby providing amazing results. After all, magick is about breaking down the barriers to the untapped regions of our minds. Psychodrama found in most rituals helps such a process along, but so does actually feeling something magickal occurring. The pull is just such a feeling.

Expanding your awareness and use of the simple pull sensation can greatly enhance the mind dowsing process. In fact, in time it's not really necessary to raise a finger and move it through the air over imaginary representations of possible answers. Once you've isolated the true essence of the pull feeling, you can let it come forth as you quickly cycle through yes/no or other possible responses. But this is only possible once you've found how the pull makes your entire body feel.

You need to isolate the connection that the pull has to emotional energy—the driving force of magick.

Rituals and psychic practices all feel a little different, depending on the circumstances surrounding them, but they all have a common core, too. They all establish a link to the mystical parts of the mind and all touch the unseen energy that connects us. In the case of magick rituals, you blast that energy off to the task of fueling some thoughtform. In psychic practice or mind reading you access that energy field to sense any information carried by it or any disruptions found within it. Mind reading makes use of both information decoding and disruption sensing.

Because psychic information is connected to the energy of the ether—the same stuff of which emotional energy is made—the pull is something that you can sense with your entire being. Your entire being is, after all, infused with mystical energy or lifeforce. Knowing how to detect energy changes enables you to use your entire body and mind as a dowsing tool.

Enough theory for now, however. Try the following with a friend:

Experiment One

Ask your friend to think of a number from one to three, and to firmly see and keep this number in mind.

Close your eyes and visualize a triangle. Assign the numbers one through three to the points. See each assigned number just within each angle or just outside each point—your choice.

Now focus on each number, one at a time. Wait for one of them to bring about a minor rush—kind of like the first stirrings of an energy-raising step in a ritual.

That number is the one your friend's thinking of.

How'd you do? If you've had some practice at raising emotional energy, you should know how to sense its presence instantly. When you succeed at the experiment a few times, with different people acting as your training subjects, try moving to the use of a square symbol, with the points corresponding to the numbers one through four.

By increasing the sizes of these symbols you can experiment with putting multiple numbers or letters in each of the angles found within them. Say you wanted to choose from the numbers one through nine. You can practice putting one through three, four through six, and seven through nine in the corners of a triangle. Then, you could try to sense which group that the thought of item is within. Say it's four through six. To hone in on the right item, you could disperse these three numbers to the corners of the symbol. You can even change the symbols used to house the characters or digits midway through an experiment, and mix in other visualizations to keep your mind focused and perhaps entertained. For instance:

Experiment Two

Ask a friend to think of a number from one to ten.

Close your eyes and visualize a pentagram—just the star itself, no circle. Mentally place two digits in each point (one and two in the top point, and so on).

Either focus on each point for a second or two to wait for a sensation, or rotate the star in your mind to bring "up" each point.

When you've got it narrowed to two numbers in one point, mentally pull them above the pentagram and focus on one number at a time to see which one makes your energy rush seem to peak.

Two notes here. First, visualizations "like" to be moved, so to speak, so rotating the pentagram symbol might yield excellent results in focusing your concentration.

Second, energy rushes come in various degrees. You may have noticed this in some rituals where you raise power to a certain level at first and then later on peak at a specific point in a rite. When narrowing down your subject's thought-of choices with your entire body like this, you'll be waiting for the peak to indicate which thought is correct.

Once you have a few freeform successes at the preceding experiments, try them both with your eyes open. Try to see the glyphs before you. After all, we can't have you walking around with your eyes closed trying to read minds, can we?

Did you succeed at still seeing the choices and feeling the emotional energy raise with your eyes open? Great, then try:

Experiment Three

Ask a friend to think of a letter.

Visualize, with your eyes open, that the alphabet is written out in a line before you. Don't worry if your open-eyed visualization doesn't yet let you see each letter beautifully written out. At least be aware of where each letter is in the line, and don't worry so much about the clarity of the font.

Move your focus from left to right over the imaginary letters. Sort of feel yourself moving through the alphabet, if you get what I mean. Don't be concerned if the letters blur. Don't worry if at some point you only know that you're, for instance, more than halfway through, but don't know at exactly which letter you've arrived. Just move through the alphabet as if it were a stick on which you were looking for a particular spot.

Go back and forth over it like this a couple of times, imaginarily feeling your way through the letters.

Eventually you'll notice that the energy within you begins to swell at a certain area.

Try to visualize which letters you are over at this point and narrow down as best you can. A letter will either leap out at you, or you'll have to slowly move over a couple to figure out which one results in a pull or peak.

Working with a friend through all of these techniques and getting instant feedback will do more than boost your ego. It will identify to your subconscious exactly which feelings are the ones you should equate with getting "warmer," so to speak.

Now, on to applying this awakening intuition in the real world at night.

Grabbing Thoughts

To get information from someone's mind without his or her knowledge usually requires the use of suggestion. You have to get someone thinking along a certain line, within certain parameters, so you can separate the desired information from the chaos that is the mind.

This is *usually* the case.

To sum up, you should work with suggestion when it's necessary to dowse within a set group of parameters, be they answers to binary, three-part, or even multipart questions—yes/no, breakfast/lunch/dinner, or a specific color of the rainbow, for instance. And the evolved form of mind dowsing you just learned will work to enhance such mind dowsing. There's no need for me to go into specifics other than to say that you can now just feel which part of a binary or multipart answer the other person is thinking of. Just see the "yes" and "no" floating, for instance, and feel which one is right. Suggest that a particular person in a five-person group would be great at a job and see which your subject individual would choose by putting the faces of the choices in a pentacle. You get the idea. Know what the possible responses are, and dowse them with your entire body.

But what if you do want to probe the chaos? What if you have no idea what the possible choices are? There is a way to edge into such practice. First, however, try this evolved use of visualized glyphs:

Psychic TV

Choose a friend to work with if you want instant feedback, or try this in a real-world setting with an unwary subject.

With eyes open, imagine a small, floating silver square in the air before you. This should be tiny enough to fit on your subject's forehead, but don't see it there just yet. For now, don't look at the subject at all.

Instead of planting a suggestion on your subject as you'd normally do, plant one on yourself. Before looking at the subject, gaze at the little psychic TV screen of sorts and silently tell yourself:

Filter of the unseen, reveal inner thoughts to me.

Immediately turn to your subject. Without planting a suggestion about the question you have in mind, see the floating screen on the subject's forehead.

Ask a question in some form to yourself and quickly see each of the possible responses in the silver field. You can see each answer as either a little symbol or picture, or black letters or numbers.

Whichever one produces the pull is likely the answer.

Notice I said "likely the answer." This technique takes a little practice. But it will work, and will prepare you for this:

I Know What You're Thinking

Use either a friend or an unwary subject.

See the psychic TV screen in the air before you, and use the suggestion:

Window to the unseen, reveal inner thoughts to me.

"Place" the screen on your subject's forehead, but do not think of a question.

Quickly raise emotional energy and note the first impression, image, word, or sensation that you receive through the psychic TV.

Immediately turn away to decipher the information you received.

That rite contains a lot of power described in few words. What's happening in it? So far, you've been training yourself to be in a receptive state when you sense the presence of emotional energy. By turning the process around on itself—by raising emotional energy on your own—you force a quick surge of reception.

It's kind of like sympathetic magick. Raise the feeling you associate with a correct answer, and you will get a correct answer.

Now, these techniques don't really replace the combination of suggestion and mind dowsing. At certain times and in certain noisy settings, you might find mind dowsing to be much easier to implement than these techniques of pulling thoughts.

The tools are yours to use how and when you desire, however.

Chapter Five

Expanding Your Intuition

Pulling thoughts and other information from the ether of night is possible. You have done this when reading minds at night—truly the best time for such practice. You have also seen evidence of this capability when listening to the night for inspiration.

Information freely travels the dark ether, both because there is less psychic interference than during the day and because the darkness sympathetically links to the essence of dreams and uninhibited thoughts. Here are some advanced ways to take advantage of this wonderful property of night—of how its ether acts as a network of thoughts.

Thoughts from Afar

You need not be in the same room or even town as the person whose mind you wish to read. As long as you're within a time zone or two of each other, there is a way to glean from his or her subconscious both the answers to your questions and various random thoughts.

First, how to find a specific answer.

Decide on whose mind you wish to scan, and the exact question you wish to ask. If you can phrase it to have one of a few predetermined responses—yes/no, red/blue/green, and so on—so much the better. If not, however, don't worry.

Make sure that both you and your subject are within psychic quiet time (3 to 5 A.M.) in your respective time zones. Have a picture of or personal item belonging to your subject handy. If these are not available, at least write his or her name on a piece of paper.

Proceed as follows:

Questioning the Dreamer

Light a black or silver candle.

Do a banishing if you know one and begin to achieve some inner quiet.

Pick up the picture, object, or paper on which you wrote the person's name. While holding this link object, close your eyes and say the person's name out loud.

Open your eyes and try to imagine the person sleeping. See him or her as a Barbie doll-sized figure lying on the table before you. If you're using a picture, it's okay to glance at it to help remember the details. When the image is complete, rest your hand holding the link object against this mental construct. Allow the link object to penetrate the etheric figure by the feet.

Know that you are actually seeing this person sleeping. Make the visualization as real-looking as possible with your eyes open.

Say the person's name again, with eyes open, and ask your question of the figure.

If your question has predetermined answers, imagine these written on the figure's forehead one at a time. See which one results in a pull or rush. That is your answer.

If your question is open ended, state it and imagine the little silver psychic TV screen on your subject's forehead. Raise some emotional energy and note the impressions that come to you.

Once you've obtained the answer using either method, allow the figure to dissipate.

Do another banishing.

What if you just want to get a glimpse of some of the issues plaguing an individual? Sometimes random thoughts picked up at psychic quiet time help us understand better where someone's "coming from."

To read from a stream of another's thoughts, gather all that you did for the last technique and proceed as follows:

Spying by Night

Light a candle.

> Do a banishing if you know one and achieve inner quiet.
>
> Pick up the link object, close your eyes, and say the person's name.
>
> Open your eyes and create a mental image of the sleeping person.

Rest your hand holding the link object against the feet of the figure.

> See the psychic TV against the phantom figure's forehead. Say:
>> *Window to the unseen, reveal inner thoughts to me.*

Raise emotional energy and allow yourself to gather the many thoughts that come to you. Try to limit this to four or five minutes, however, to prevent the loss of vital information due to your own boredom.

> Allow the figure to dissipate.
>
> Do another banishing.

Intuiting from All Around You

The more you work with mind reading of all types and with listening to the night, the more your general intuition will sharpen. In time, you won't need to seek out useful information; information will come to you when it will be most useful.

How can this be? Again, night facilitates the easy travel of information, some from the living and dead, some from the Gods. The more you practice drawing from night any knowledge you need for a particular reason, the more your subconscious learns how to do this automatically. Training your intuition to work for you is kind of like learning how to touch type. First you think of each finger movement to get the desired letter. In time, however, the words will just appear on the screen before you like magick.

Your subconscious is learning how to automatically pick out information that's useful to you. We're all born with some degree of this filtering, which is all that intuition really is. The problem is that few of us pay attention to the data that our subconscious filters and gathers for us out of the realm of thought.

Now that your mind is becoming attuned to such intelligence gathering, do not make the mistake of ignoring all the hard work it's doing for you. Listen to it, whenever you can. You can do this in nonritualistic ways throughout your days and particularly your nights. If you get a bad feeling about something or decide to go a different way than usual on a routine trip, follow your instincts. If a certain item catches your eye, consider for a moment if it might be a symbol of some significance—if the item is trying to tell you something.

Look for coincidences. Look for things you've been thinking of that just happen to manifest thereafter. Such events might have significance from which you will be able to glean valuable lessons.

In addition to just trusting your gut about things, try the following:

Attracting Intuition

Perform a banishing if you know one and do your best to achieve inner quiet.

With your eyes closed, look to the upper left of your inner dark field. It's okay to lift your head up in that direction a bit, to add to the feeling that you're trying to physically see toward the upper left.

Take a deep breath, and tense to raise emotional energy.

As you exhale, release the tensed energy and visualize in the upper left, with your eyes closed, a flash of red light. Don't worry if the color is not vibrant. Only know it's there, and know it's there because you sent out energy to make it be so.

Continuing to breathe with the same deep rhythm, use your next inhaling and exhaling cycle to move your inner vision down and to the right a bit. That is, breathe in while moving your inner gaze, and exhale while fixing the new spot in your mind. To gauge how far down the move should be, consider that you will be moving to a total of seven such positions, ending at the lower right corner of your inner field of vision.

On your next inhalation, tense and raise energy. Exhale, releasing the energy and visualizing a flash of orange. Again, just know that it's happening if you don't see it clearly.

Move down and to the right on your next breathing cycle.

Repeat the charged visualization with a yellow flash. Then go on to alternately move diagonally down and raise energy to see each of the other rainbow colors you know are coming: green, then blue, indigo, and violet.

After seeing violet, continue to breathe deeply for three cycles.

Then take one extra-deep breath, tensing stronger than you did for each of the colors in the cycle. Raise up as startling a blast of energy as you can, and say, out loud:

The answer to my next question will come to me this night.

Count to three out loud and open your eyes.

Immediately ask yourself a question.

Venture out into the night and live. Pay attention. You'll be amazed at how soon you'll have an answer.

The answers you receive by doing this simple rite may not always be obvious. However, intuition has a peculiar way of developing. As it gets better, your intuition will point out better symbols and the like for you to interpret.

As an encyclopedic listing of symbols won't help you much at all, I won't provide one. The symbols that appear to you will be personal ones that only you can glean meaning from—otherwise, your subconscious wouldn't notice them! Most symbols, even so-called "universal" ones, just won't mean the same things to different people.

In addition to pointing out more symbols and more meaningful ones to you in time, your intuition will also get faster and more independent with practice. You won't always need to find too many outside symbols to answer the concerns you have. Much as inspiration just comes to you when listening to the night, intuitive answers to the questions you have in life will just enter your mind.

Try the following:

Rapid Blasts of Inspiration

Consider a question that has been plaguing you for some time and break it up into issues of past, present, and future. For instance, if you're in debt and need help, think about how you got into debt, what you can do to better the situation right now, and how you can ensure better control of your money in the future.

Do a banishing if possible and attain some inner quiet.

With your eyes open, imagine a large triangle. Know that each of the triangle's points represents one of the three aforementioned aspects of your problem.

Start with the past as the top point. Gaze just inside the angle, meditate for a few seconds on what the point represents, and raise emotional energy. Record or note somehow what appears or comes to you. A tape recorder or scratch pad might be handy if you want to remain relaxed and not worry about remembering symbols.

When you're sure you fully received your insight—be it a symbol, word, or abstract thought—move on. Rotate the triangle clockwise 120 degrees and know that the next point to come up has to do with the present.

Gaze and raise energy again. Note any insight about the present that comes to you.

Rotate the triangle one last time to get to the point concerning the future.

Look for a symbol or inspiration as you raise some energy one last time. Record your insight.

Do not do a banishing when you're done. Spend some time going over the symbols to see what they mean to you.

Think of these techniques as triggers for stirring up something that you've always had, and which has already begun getting active. Some of the other things you try in this grimoire will take advantage of your intuition, too.

Closing Your Mind to Others

As your mind expands in its ability to reach out and snatch the data it needs, you should become exceedingly aware of just how much freely floating data is out there. Our minds are in many ways open books, so to speak. Most of us are more in tune with each other than we believe ourselves to be . . . not always a good thing.

Just as you're learning to open yourself to the knowledge with which the night is pregnant, I'm also going to recommend you learn to close yourself off.

No, there aren't mind readers running rampant trying to steal all your inner thoughts. Don't think for a minute that the government or some other agency has teams of them probing you to see what you're up to. As you've seen, mind reading is not something you can use to blanket scan a bunch of people. Our interconnected network of thoughts is not quite that easily decipherable en masse.

But, as I said, everyone has intuition. Your inner thoughts might be secure from most people as far as word-for-word probing of them is concerned, but the gist of what you're thinking might come across to more people more often than you think.

It's dangerous, too, letting people pick up on magickal thought-forms that you want to create. You don't really want to talk about them, as people can build up their own thoughtforms to counter the ones you create. Hiding your thoughts in general makes the blocking of your goals and thoughtforms impossible for others to do.

Also, there will come times where you're certain someone is "on to you," so to speak. As you deal with more and more occult folk, you will come across those who seem to know a bit too much about you. Not to invoke any kind of paranoia here, but some people get off on being perceived as all-knowing about you. Encountering such people may make you uncomfortable, unless you're confident that you're shut-down.

For a variety of reasons, some of which I had better let you supply, you should consider practicing closing off your thoughts. If for no other reason, it helps you build up power. The less psychic clutter you send out to the ether of night, the easier outside data will be able to get in amidst the silence that surrounds you.

Steps to Mind Cloaking

Know that for the most part your will is always obeyed by the universe. This is even more the case when you're dealing with control over your mind. Know, in other words, that if you will your mind to be closed to probing often enough, it will learn to automatically close itself to probing.

Think on this fact every night if possible, at least for a month.

Also, for the same period of time, practice the following nightly.

Achieve some inner quiet—even by trying for a mere minute.

Visualize an etheric egg-shaped shield floating around you. It is noticeably different on the inside and outside layers.

The inside layer is silver and reflective. Meditate on this for a moment and think about how your inner thoughts will reflect back to you, bouncing around within your aura and building energy.

Raise some emotional energy and say:

Only the Gods of night may know my inner thoughts.

The inner layer should seem more real now.

Focus on the outer layer of the egg shield. See that it is black. Meditate on how this black layer will not only allow filtered thoughts to enter, but will actually pull desired thoughts to you.

Raise some emotional energy and say:

The knowledge I seek shall always flow freely to me.

The outer layer should seem more solid.

Go on with your night, knowing that the barrier and filter is always around you.

After doing the aforementioned rite for a month, you will only need to repeat it every few months or so to reaffirm to your subconscious that you are in control of the flow of information both to and from your mind.

Should you ever feel yourself under an unusual amount of scrutiny, try the following:

A Quick Seal

Become aware of the thought shield around you.

Quickly raise emotional energy and say to yourself:

My thoughts veiled, my will undaunted.

If you can detect who is trying to probe you, close your eyes and imagine a gray cloud the size of a basketball floating a few feet away from you, but in the direction of the person.

See that the gray cloud has little silver sparks crackling within it.

Open your eyes, look at the form you built up before you, and send an optical blast of emotional energy to it, saying to yourself:

If my thoughts he (or she) seeks, let confusion be found instead.

Let the cloud drift toward the person, but don't see it surrounding his or her head. Look away, knowing that the form will only act if it needs to.

Chapter Six

Divining the Dark Signs

Symbols are only meaningful to those who interpret them. As I've said, the fact that a symbol stands out to you at all means that it has meaning for you. In working with general intuition, you may have found symbols to take some strange forms and appear to you in even stranger ways. As we'll get to in a bit, these symbols that just seem to manifest may even coalesce into overwhelming omens with the help of certain prevalent nocturnal life forms and phenomena.

However, we can also try to group symbols together on our own when we need to find answers from our intuition. As you did in chapter 5 when assigning a visualized triangle with points regarding past, present, and future, you can organize symbols to tell a complete story. And these don't have to be abstract symbols whose appearance you must await.

They can be symbols you deal out by candlelight onto a table before you.

Tarot for Nightkind

It may come as a real shock to some occult purists when they first real-ize that there is no set "right" way to read tarot. Much as recent evi-dence seems to indicate that this portable oracle did not come to us from ancient Egypt, careful study of tarot history reveals that the sym-bols and even particular cards have changed numerous times over the years. Decks have not always had the so-called standard seventy-eight cards, for instance, and many still don't. Some decks have Kabalistic or astrological significance added to them, some are forced into corre-sponding with other aspects of nature. Some decks are attributed to Gods and Goddesses. None of these associations can be proven to be older than a century or two.

The first cards might have been nothing more than a gaming device. We don't know for sure.

What we do know, however, is that when designed by someone who is attuned to using his or her intuition, a deck can be a very mag-ickal portal to accessing our own intuition. Assuming, of course, that the inspired tool inspires us.

You might already have a tarot deck that you can begin working with. Did you choose such a deck because its imagery and symbolism spoke to you on some level? Then this deck will be an excellent divina-tory tool. However, if this is an old deck you had lying around but could never seem to get to work for readings, it might be time to go shopping.

There are plenty of decks available that will appeal, at least some-what, to the sensibilities of nightkind. I'm a big fan of *The Secret Tarots* by Marco Nizzoli. Just make certain that whichever deck you pick has illustrated pips (actual imagery incorporating the two of swords, five of pentacles, and so on). It's crucial to the method of reading cards you're about to learn that all the cards contain some kind of pictures for your intuition to explore. Simply staring at a couple of swords, for instance, won't provide enough symbolism to work with.

Also, when choosing an appropriately dark deck, you will want to stay away from anything that seems too . . . contrived? That is, any decks that seem made by gaming companies to take advantage of the popularity of, say, beings like vampires. Make sure such a deck isn't really just a repetitive series of shock imagery that you almost can't differentiate. For example, vampire drinks from a woman's neck in one card, drinks from her neck's other side in another, and all against a black background. You get the idea, I'm sure. Make sure that the deck has some occult reason for being, according to your intuition, and enough diversity in its imagery to inspire you.

When you think you've found the right deck, consider doing a dedication for it in a magick circle. Use this simple rite:

Dedicating the Deck

Cast a circle.

Pick up the deck in your two upturned palms. Hold the cards in front of the nocturnal portal.

Angle your hands so you can see the deck's reflection in your skrying tool. See how the cards are surrounded by a charged, glowing darkness, much as what you see when skrying.

Still looking into the portal, imagine that the nocturnal energy around the deck is slowly seeping into the cards themselves. Feel this happening at all sides of the deck; feel the energy moving around your hands (but keep your eyes on the portal). Say:

I dedicate you, creatures of paper, to the service of the Gods and Goddesses of Night.
Allow me to pull from your faces the symbols and knowledge I
seek in answer to my queries.
So mote it be.

Pass the deck through the censer's smoke for a silent count of three.

Never use the cards for mundane purposes again. Keep them in a pouch of black silk if possible—or at least black cloth—until they are needed.

You're now ready to begin working with the cards. If you've already shuffled them, return the cards to the order in which they are listed in the book or booklet that comes with the deck, with the first card faceup on top. You can read the book or booklet at some point if you like, but for now you will only use its card description section. You'll also need a pen and a notebook containing about 160 pages.

Getting to Know Them

Look at the first card in your deck (likely the Fool or its equivalent). Write its name at the top of the first page of the notebook.

Read the description of the card's meaning. Write down the parts of the meaning that make sense to you. If you see how the card represents irresponsibility, for example, write this word in your notebook, or write a sentence explaining the concept—whatever moves you.

Ignore for now whichever meanings of the card you don't seem to see for yourself and write nothing about them.

Add to the page any meanings that the symbols in the card seem to indicate to you. Make sure you allow at least one such thought to come to you, even if it's just a combination of some of the thoughts you already read in the booklet.

Rotate the card so that the image is on its head. Read in the deck's book any meanings for the card when it's inverted or reversed. If none are listed, look at the meanings you already wrote in your notebook and think about what they might mean in lesser or incomplete degrees. For example, "moderation" might translate to "still prone to occasional excessive behavior." Inverted cards are simply indicative of energies that are present to a lesser degree, and which may grow in intensity.

Turn what should still be at least a half-empty page to the next empty one (only write on the right-hand pages, to make skimming for cards easy), and turn over the card, facedown, next to the deck.

Write the name of the next card on the next right-hand page and repeat the process.

Do this for a few cards per sitting. After going in order a couple of times (maybe after you've done ten cards or so, total), feel free to label all the right-hand pages in your notebook with the card names, in order, and then jump around from card to card in future sittings.

You should eventually go through all the cards this way and return to ones you've done from time to time.

However, after having done only ten cards or so within a few sittings, you can start doing readings. The reason you can start before getting through the whole deck is simple. The process just described is not one of memorization. Note that I am not asking you to really commit to memory the meanings of the cards. The meanings that truly make sense to you will "stick" in time. Even the meanings of cards you haven't yet meditated on will come to you in a reading.

Again, the purists may chime in here. The cards have set meanings, they say. The meanings are universal and eternal. Whatever. The only time multiple decks have cards with similar meanings is arguably when said multiple decks are influenced by the Rider-Waite deck.

Do the card meditations for the whole deck. It is a good intuition-trainer, the process of adding an interpretation to the card pages and omitting the meanings that don't make sense to you. However, it is no substitution for letting your intuition apply the symbols of a card within the context of a reading. Again, much as when you assigned past, present, and future to the points of a triangle glyph, you're about to assign card symbols to specific aspects of a question.

And, at no point in a reading, ever, should you look up a card's meaning—even in your notebook. Trust the night's influence and your intuition to help you deal out cards that will mean something to you. Looking up a card's meaning during a reading can temporarily cripple or shut down intuition. Your subconscious will have no reason to help you if you're just going to take the path of least resistance anyway.

So, when doing your first or hundredth reading, make sure that putting your notebook away is step one.

Countless books contain instructions for the Celtic Cross spread. I won't be giving that one here. If you're used to it, stick with it. If you like the idea of using the spread most people use, seek it out.

The spread we'll be using encourages you to spend more time skrying fewer cards. Wait, did you read that right? Yes, I said "skrying" the cards. You wouldn't want to trust the symbolism of a card to tell the whole story, would you?

The Nocturnal Spread

Whether reading for yourself or another, try to use candlelight and incense to set up a suitable atmosphere. This is not just for mood, either. Remember, you will be attempting to skry the surface of the cards. If reading for someone else, he or she should be seated across from you.

Perform a quick banishing when seated at the table. Spend a moment achieving some inner quiet.

The person asking the question should pick up the deck, hold it in his or her hands, and ask aloud about a particular area of life. Usually money or love queries are most popular, followed by health, then other issues that are less frequently encountered.

Make sure the person making the query thinks of the question and any people or events associated with it in as neutral a manner as possible. For example, if a woman is asking about finding a mate, make sure she thinks of how nice it would be to find one, and maybe some of the traits he should possess. She should not think about how nice it would be to hook up with a particular person. If the questioner thinks too specifically about something, it will manifest as wish fulfillment in the cards. So, unless the person wants advice on how to get so and so interested in him or her—a far different reading than one about finding a mate in general—the questioner should make sure all thoughts match the question.

The questioner should shuffle the cards while holding any appropriate thoughts in mind as best as he or she can. A hand-over-hand shuffle should be used. Every time the end of the deck is reached in this manner, the deck should be cut and one half should be rotated 180 degrees (to make some of the cards inverted). Then the shuffling should resume.

Repeat the shuffle, cut, and rotate at least three times, and for as long as it takes for the shuffle to feel "right" to the questioner.

If you're reading for someone else, take the cards before you, facedown. Rotate them so that they're oriented to you as they would have been to the questioner.

Have the questioner concentrate one last time on what he or she is asking and tell him or her to cut the deck.

Place the bottom pile of the cut cards on top of the other pile and prepare to deal cards off the deck's new top.

Close your eyes and try to strengthen your state of inner quiet. Say quietly or even to yourself:

The unseen world is readily open to me.

My inner sight is true and far reaching.

Open your eyes and deal out the Nocturnal Pentagram Spread (Figure 6–1) in the numbered order shown. Leave each card facedown and oriented or rotated as it was on the pile.

The last card—card six, the center card—should not be dealt until the end of the reading.

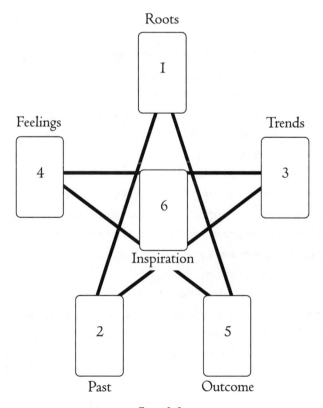

Figure 6–1

Turn over the first card—Roots—by its side so as to not change its orientation.

Think about the question at hand and gaze at the card. This card represents the root of the question—the issues directly affecting the person asking it. Allow any immediate impressions to come to you based on what you think the card means. Use your intuition first, then skry.

Contemplating the root of the questioner's concern, allow yourself to achieve the feeling you get when skrying. Pick a part of the card that has a uniform field of color and allow your vision to sink into it. Then, when you feel your developed ability kicking in, move your gaze over the surface of the card. Look for symbols that seem to animate and draw attention to themselves, or look for images that appear on the card as open-eyed hallucinations. Trust your intuition—it will give you the right symbols to focus on, even if the deck didn't contain them in the first place!

Another phenomenon to watch for is when a part of the card "opens up" and reveals a vision of what the person did or should do, or of what the possible outcome is. Every reading will vary, but with practice you will see a great deal when looking into the cards.

After you're done assimilating your impressions, both instant and skryed, try to explain your understanding of the root card aloud to the questioner in a relaxed tone.

Turn over the second card: Past.

See what immediate inspiration comes to you regarding the card's symbolism and how it applies to the past issues surrounding the question. Then skry as before. With all this information gathered, relay your understanding of it to the questioner.

Turn over the third card: Trends.

Interpret the symbols and skryed visions you have, considering that this card represents the general trends currently moving with or against the questioner and the issue at hand. Explain your findings.

Turn over the fourth card: Feelings.

Repeat the process of looking for inspiration and skrying, this time considering the questioner's feelings—maybe hopes and fears—about the issue. Relay what you learn. Exploring these feelings helps prepare the questioner to hear about the future.

Turn over the fifth card: Outcome.

Explain whatever symbolism seems relevant to the question's outcome. Note that if you're to have a vision within the card's surface at anytime during this reading, now is the time it will most likely happen. Not only because you've been skrying for a while by this point in a reading, but also because most people come to a reading looking for a clear vision of the future. Your subconscious knows this and will try at this point to provide just such a glimpse.

Add the sixth card to the spread, turning it faceup as you do so. This card represents something about the reading that the Gods of Night wish you to note. Interpret it with this in mind, and look to see if there are any other visions awaiting your notice.

One final note on readings. Do not "insult" your intuition by immediately reading about the same question again. At times during the reading you may uncover something that the questioner should be doing to better his or her situation. If you pass on this information and the person acts on it, then you can soon read again concerning the same issue. Otherwise, wait at least a few weeks to allow some of the forces involved to play out and present you with new information.

Don't let your intuition feel like it is a mere casual entertainment for you. Treat it with the respect it deserves as a growing tool in your mystical consciousness.

Dark Omens

If you've been opening yourself to the darkness and listening to it, you no doubt learned that inspiration can come from the ether in strange ways. Now, with your work in interpreting symbols progressing as well, the universe may deign to begin sharing inspiration and information with you in the form of omens.

Nocturnal omens might come to you in the guise of things you notice at night—perhaps those things that the light of the moon draws you to notice—or even in the form of the creatures that are, themselves, sympathetic links to darkness.

Again, I'm not a fan of telling others what symbols mean to them, so this section will not be an encyclopedic listing of symbols. Rather, we'll look at the two types of omens most likely to enter your awareness.

Moonlit Signs

Much as the letters of the alphabet can be arranged into countless words and phrases, any visible object can be added to another to make a statement. In the case of non-living symbols (we'll get to living ones in a moment), when the night gathers a few of them to your attention, it is an omen you should not ignore.

If a patch of moonlight happens to break through the trees and hits a coin on the ground, for instance, it might mean that money is coming your way. However, if said illuminated coin is followed a few seconds later by you dropping something that's important to you into a dark patch of bushes, then maybe the universe is trying to tell you something else. Be careful how you hang on to money in the future, perhaps?

Also watch for numbers. Sometimes you'll have a question that's plaguing you and a number would help you determine the answer. For example, what percentage of your paycheck should you be saving? Be on the lookout for either a number written as part of something else that stands out to you, or a collection of dark rocks that seems to add up to a proper number.

This kind of thing will happen often, but don't take my word for it. See for yourself, literally.

Much as you have been keeping aware of your intuition and the insights it brings you throughout the night, keep watch for collections of symbols. If they are meant for you, you'll get them. Don't worry about that.

Creatures of Night

The most amazing nocturnal omens are the ones that actually come right to you, or that pass in front of or over you. And they don't have to manifest in pairs or greater numbers—even one creature of night can act as an indisputable omen.

Now, by creature of night I'm not just referring to an animal that keeps nocturnal hours; those beings, such as bats and owls, certainly do make up part of our definition—but also be on the lookout for animals that have sympathetic links to darkness. Maybe the animal is black, or maybe it does something that links it to one of the types of nocturnal deities, or maybe it's even a symbol of a God or Goddess itself.

Synthesizing all the possibilities, we can generalize and state that there are three basic types of creature that can bring a nocturnal omen to you. They are those animals that (a) thrive at night; (b) mirror night; or (c) represent night's deities.

Bats, owls, raccoons, and a variety of other small animals make nighttime their preferred hours of hunting and living. That they thrive at night means they are naturally attuned to its currents. Although they do not understand that they are coexisting with a time that is almost sentient, they do pick up on the energies of the ether. Do not be surprised, therefore, if one of these creatures appears to you at a time when you are waiting for the ether itself to provide inspiration. You will have to interpret how an owl's four hoots, for instance, answer the question for which you're listening to the night, but an answer it just may be. Of course, if you come across one of these creatures by daylight—a very uncommon and therefore significant event—it may have an even more urgent message to share with you, so pay extra attention to its actions and how it appears.

Animals that mirror night can appear at any time. Ravens and crows are the ones you'll notice most often, if they're indigenous to your area. And if they're not found where you live, something extremely mysterious is afoot should one appear! As carrion eaters, crows and ravens have mythically been associated with carrying dead souls. While I don't believe that they serve such a purpose, I do believe that the thoughtforms surrounding them have helped them take on extra mystical power, much like the Sabbats or nights of power have built up potency over the years. I once met a man who looked to crows for answers to many important questions. He would do this by citing how many of them appeared, how many departed, and what shapes they landed in. If you find these or other black creatures vying for your attention by day or night, consider that there might be a motive to their strange behavior.

The final type of nocturnal creature is one that has been associated with a deity. In the case of the Old Gods of Egypt, these associations are quite obvious, being that the heads of the deities were actually those of animals. If you're questioning whether to summon the dead to physical appearance and encounter a jackal, for instance, chances are that Anubis is smiling on your desire. Other nocturnal deities, however, require a little digging and research. If you've been reading myths and correspondences surrounding deities before trying to invoke them, then you've already come across animals that are either sacred to the Gods you love or are forms they've appeared as in legend. Next time you see such a sacred creature of night, consider: Are the Gods that you often call on trying to reach out to you?

Part Three

Moving Unseen
and Making Them See

Chapter Seven

Astral Travel

Practicing magick brings you into greater contact with the unseen energies of the universe. While you've been tapping this lifeforce for all your life, you are now, no doubt, consciously aware of its existence. Are you also aware of the form that this energy resides in while lurking within you?

Coexisting with the physical plane on the astral one, lifeforce energy fuels our astral bodies. Lifeforce comes to us from the ether, but we also create it. This lifeforce is the astral double of the energy that our life processes create and burn to sustain us. Astral energy is static and clings to us, awaiting our direction and use of it.

Recall that all magick occurs on the mental, then astral, then physical planes. Our connection to the mental plane in life is our trained mind and, in death, our very soul. Our thoughts planted on the mental plane take form on the astral one eventually. In much the same progressing fashion, our very consciousness can take control of our own astral form. Our mental consciousness or souls can, at will (and only with mystical will), leave our physical bodies while encased in the astral forms we all possess.

Of course we're talking of astral projection, or out-of-body experiences. Taking part in such etheric travel has proven for many people that we can survive physical death, yet it can also be a great tool for experiencing the magickal realms that we strive to manipulate with our workings. Moving about astrally, you will see thoughtforms, mystical entities, the dead, and all manner of phenomena just outside the realm of our ordinary perception.

On that note, it's important to recognize that while you are out of body you will not really be traveling in the physical world as we know it. While some of it will look the same, you will be seeing it with astral eyes. That is, much as you strain while in your physical body to see the astral world as it really is, you will find it difficult while in the astral form to discern your physical surroundings clearly. Some objects you see will really be there, but some will be ones that have only been thought of at this point.

Note that I'm using the word "will" a lot. That's because you *will* get out of your body with the technique you're about to learn.

The "How" Behind the Experience

To leave the physical body really only requires two steps—two steps in the occult mechanics of the process, that is. It will seem like you have to do more than two things to get out of your body, but you will eventually find that regardless of how many steps you take to accomplish them, only two actual changes occur to make the seemingly miraculous possible.

You need only sense your astral body and will it to rise. That's it, two steps.

In time, doing this two-step exit from your physical body will become quite easy. For now, you'll need to rely on a bit of your magickal experience to help you get started. While people may read books on astral travel and then try for months to have their first success at it, you'll be approaching it with the help of ritual and already developing mystical senses.

In normal consciousness our energy bodies are usually undetected by us. In ritual, we make contact with them a bit, especially during godform assumption, but mostly we just access the energy that fuels them. The ritual you'll be doing—admittedly for at least a few nights —will be programming your subconscious, through autosuggestion, to become fully aware of your subtle body. Moving out of your physical body in this shell will then require conscious will.

As we'll explore in a moment, there are a couple of ways that aware-ness of your energy body will manifest: You can either be awake or asleep when it occurs. For now, however, let's just deal with what you'll need to bring about that exciting moment when you can feel yourself on the edge of astral adventure.

The Preparatory Ritual
Wait until after sunset.

Perform a banishing if you know one and do your best to achieve inner quiet.

With your eyes closed, look to the upper left of your inner dark field (this part is similar to the color visualizations you did in chapter 5). Take a deep breath, and tense to raise emotional energy.

As you exhale, release the tensed energy and visualize in the upper left, with your eyes closed, a flash of red light.

The next time you breathe in, move your inner gaze down and to the right. Upon exhaling, fix the new spot in your mind. Remember, you're going for a total of seven such positions, so allow room for the last one to end at the lower right corner of your inner field of vision.

On your next inhalation, tense and raise energy. Exhale, releasing the energy and visualizing a flash of orange.

Move down and to the right on your next breathing cycle.

Repeat the charged visualization with a yellow flash. Then go on to alternately move diagonally down and raise energy to see each of the other rainbow colors you know are coming: green, then blue, indigo, and violet.

After seeing violet, continue to breathe deeply for three cycles.

Then take one extra-deep breath, tensing stronger than you did for each of the colors in the cycle. Raise up as startling a blast of energy as you can, and say, out loud:

Tonight I consciously leave my body.

Without opening your eyes just yet, raise as much emotional energy as you can. Feel it pulsing through you, and know that it does so because there is a more subtle "you" inside for it to run through.

As the energy is peaking, say:

> *Astral shell, awaken when I need you.*

Now, count to three out loud and open your eyes. Without thinking of what you did, try to get absorbed with another activity.

You should repeat this rite every night until you get the following "Leaving your Shell" rite to work. Once that occurs, you'll be able to do away with the elaborate Preparatory Ritual and simply repeat the two suggestion sentences from it each night, in bed, as you're readying for sleep.

Leaving your Shell

Until your first success at astral travel, make sure you perform the Preparatory Ritual at some point before (even hours before) going to sleep.

Lie down in bed when ready to travel and say the two suggestions as a couplet:

> *Tonight I consciously leave my body.*
> *Astral shell, awaken when I need you.*

Close your eyes and repeat the couplet to yourself.

Imagine that your consciousness is really a glowing silver sphere resting in your throat. Visualize this sphere and continue repeating the couplet.

Repeat the previous step (of seeing the sphere and mentally reciting the couplet) for as long as you can, but try to catch yourself right before falling asleep. If you fail, don't worry, for reasons that will become clear in a moment.

You should try to "catch yourself" at that moment when your hypnagogic visualization is at its best. At this time, imagine that you are the glowing silver sphere, and that you are no longer in your throat. This isn't astral travel yet, so don't feel pressured to experience too real a visualization all at once. Just imagine that you are the silver sphere, and that you are in, perhaps, another room in your home or in a favorite place.

Once you begin to visualize that you are the sphere, only repeat the "Tonight I consciously leave my body" line.

Continue to visualize, as best you can, this other place, and continue to mentally think of the first line of the couplet.

Occasionally, the above visualization will turn into a full out-of-body experience. You'll feel a powerful energy vibration coursing through the form you find yourself in, and will be shocked by the clarity of the experience. The vibrations are your awareness of your energy body, and the fact that you're out makes it an instant success. If this immediate form of astral travel occurs, you'll be ready to take control with the techniques taught later.

More likely, you will continue, nightly, to fall asleep during either your visualization of the sphere in another place or even before that step, while you are still repeating the full couplet. Eventually, however, a night will come when you awaken to experience either full or partial success.

Full success will manifest with you waking up out of your body, either floating against your ceiling in your room or standing by the door or even floating in another room. You will experience the vibrations just described. The only thing you'll need to do is take control (again, more on that soon).

Partial success is when you wake up still in body, but feeling the vibrations. This means you have the awareness of your energy body, but haven't achieved liftoff. You'll need to immediately remedy that.

Will yourself to rise and try one of a few things to help yourself do so. Imagine yourself floating up gently first. If this doesn't work, try rolling sideways out of your body. The immediate movement of a roll helps solidify your awareness of the new body that your consciousness inhabits. If you have a hard time getting yourself to move either of these ways, imagine yourself sitting up. Once you're half out, so to speak, the rest will follow.

As a last resort, imagine reaching up and grabbing on to the ceiling. Your astral body will bend and stretch to suit your wishes, and you may be able to pull yourself out this way (a strange sensation, but it works from time to time).

If you're finding that a month of the preceding techniques does not yield astral travel, try varying your timing. Try doing the Preparatory Ritual and setting your alarm for psychic quiet time—maybe the middle of such, or 4 A.M. Go to sleep without doing the mantras and visualizations. When your alarm awakens you, get up and move your pillow to the other side of the bed to signify you're trying something different. Now lie down and do the mantras and sphere visualization. The combination of psychic quiet time and the fact that you should be bordering on the hypnagogic state should help you have success faster.

Taking Control

However you find yourself out of your body, you may be disappointed to find yourself back in your body all too quickly. The experience feels so exciting and powerful, even to those who've done it dozens of times, that it can jolt you back to your physical body. To prevent this letdown, and get something out of what you've worked so hard to achieve, try to remember and do the following when you're out of body.

When you're first out of your body, try not to look at your physical form. Looking at it too soon might shock you back inside. You can allow yourself to glance at the physical form after you've been out for a while—that is, after you've moved around a bit. Don't worry about trying to sense how much time is passing, as time doesn't feel at all the same on the astral plane.

With attention turned away from your physical shell, make a mental affirmation, saying something like, "I am in control of my astral form."

Then, do not even think of your physical body for a while. Always think of being elsewhere, be it the opposite side of your room, another room, or even another country.

Getting around is quite easy, you'll find. You can will yourself to move in a certain direction and you shall float. You can will yourself to fly up and out of your home, and you'll fly at any speed you wish. You can also, more bizarrely, just wish yourself to manifest elsewhere—and, as if teleported, you will end up at this place.

But, again, the "somewhere" you end up will not be quite the same place in the astral as in the physical.

More now on the astral. . . .

Chapter Eight

Astral Manipulations

One of the most interesting concepts to experiment with is how your astral form interacts with the physical plane. After all, as a Witch and magickian you know that astral forms are awaiting manifestation and that they will have an eventual effect on the physical planes.

Now, your astral body will never evolve into a physical one, obviously, but by its nature it is always one step away from the physical. Willpower can therefore empower it to interact with the more tangible plane from time to time. This is basically why you can cast subtle illusions or glamoury. More on that in the next chapter.

But before worrying too much about the waking world, start with what's natural. When in an astral form, touch things on the astral plane.

The Subtle World

When out of body, look about you. You will find it's a strange world that you're floating around within. Some objects will seem alien—even those you encounter in your own bedroom. There will be odd-colored things here and there, and even stranger-shaped objects.

Now, whenever you encounter something really bizarre, try to affect it. Walk or float right up to it and give it a push. Attempt to lift it. You'll find that in many ways this odd object you choose will feel a lot like what you're used to feeling on the physical plane. It's when you encounter a physical object that things change.

Note that you can recognize, slightly, the room you are in when you first come out of body. This is not because you are truly seeing the physical walls around you, however. Any casual glancing you do will yield views of nothing but the astral thoughtforms that went into those walls being there. Now, this is important. You are not looking at the astral *bodies* of the walls, just the astral forms that helped the physical ones eventually take shape. These are not linked entities in terms of appearance. If you thought recently about painting your walls a different color, for instance, there's a chance the astral representation will already be this color.

You can try to feel the astral walls, or pass through them. It's your choice how you interact. The astral world bends to your will in most every way. You can also move through the physical walls, of course.

But what if you wish to touch and feel the physical walls, or any other physical object for that matter?

Touching the physical plane is possible, once you've experimented with touching and identifying the "stuff" that makes up the astral one. However, touching the physical requires a great amount of willpower and concentration, and might not yield the best results for months or even years.

But before you can touch a physical object, you need to will yourself to see one.

Seeing and Touching the Physical

After attaining some idea of how astral objects feel, you will begin to realize that this allows you to sense, from a distance, the astral nature of these objects. You will have no doubt, in time, as to what is astral.

The more subtle astral plane will seem, ironically, the most physical to you when you're out of body.

Even seeing a physical object is difficult, being analogous to trying to see an aura for the first time while still in your body. Seeing physical objects requires the same shifting of perception, but in reverse; an attempt to see beyond the now visually "loud" astral form and to the indistinct physical one. Fortunately, there is one object to start with that you know is devoid of astral form: your physical body. You can use sight of your physical body as a calibration exercise of sorts. The astral part of your physical body is, of course, currently not "in place."

Trying to see your physical form while out of it, however, is dangerous. As mentioned, it might shock you back inside. When trying to see your physical body, do not think of it. Only try to casually turn toward it while in the same room, and then only turn so that you will encounter your feet first. Seeing your head first might be too startling. In fact, if you start to feel "creeped-out" in any way, let your visual scanning progress no farther than your midsection. Don't worry about catching an unwanted peripheral glimpse of your head. You'll find that in the astral you can limit your vision to a small area, or expand it to something far wider than your physical vision. Use this to your advantage.

Whatever parts you feel comfortable looking at, focus on them. And I do mean *focus*. Allow your malleable astral vision to adjust itself so that your physical body becomes clearest in your vision. When this happens, note the feeling you have. Changing your focus will have an effect on the "frequency" of your malleable astral body. Tell yourself that you can automatically adjust to such vision by trying to imagine the change of vibration. More immediately, try to maintain this focus as you turn quickly to some object of which you know the location. Try to see that object you chose, resting in its rightful place and in only its physical form.

You can now experiment with trying to touch the physical counterpart of the things around you.

One of the most important things you'll be mastering is control. By not allowing yourself to pop back into your physical body during all your experimental focus on the physical plane, you'll be learning how to maintain your astral form for extended periods of time.

Mainly, your practice will consist of identifying something physical, using your body as a visual calibration again if necessary. When certain that you have a physical object in sight, you can practice reaching out one astral finger and poking it. Imagine as you do so, however, that your finger vibrates in that slightly different way you detected when shifting your visual focus. Actually, it should more than vibrate at that frequency. In your mind, your finger should be emanating such vibrations out to the universe.

I'll let you imagine the possibilities of success in such an endeavor. For if you touch such an object, who knows? With enough willpower, you might be able to move it.

Astral Magick

As difficult as it can be to move physical objects with your astral body, the practice is one I've found to be excellent for trying to expand control over the astral body. With enough practice at even just trying to touch physical objects, you'll find that you can in a sense solidify your place in the astral world and spend long amounts of time there.

But this astral telekinesis of sorts, even if you succeed at it, won't really provide you with a great way to make changes to the physical world. And that's what magick most often provides the tools to do—create change.

If you'd like to use your astral experiences to create notable changes to the physical or waking world, you may want to consider doing some of your magick while out of body.

This might be one of the shortest subsections in this grimoire. The point is to not introduce you to a new magickal technique—just a new set of surroundings to try magick within. In particular, you will find thoughtform creation to be particularly powerful while out of body.

It is the astral plane, after all, that gives form to thoughtforms. When out of body, you can create an astral form and charge it to a specific goal, all without casting a circle and performing an invocation.

Decide on a statement that defines what your thoughtform is, and use your visualization to both mold it out of the surrounding astral ether and to imagine the final outcome of the form.

Then see your thoughtform launch off into the ether, in a way you could never do with open-eyed visualization on the physical plane.

And see how quickly your desires manifest on the physical plane!

Bizarre Places and Encounters

From time to time, an out-of-body experience will take you someplace you never knew existed. This could be an odd building or room or some weird temple of sorts. It could be a fantasy-type forest or a desert with odd-colored sand. You're not always going to end up in a place that even remotely resembles the physical plane. Some places still only exist on the astral plane. However, it doesn't mean you can't learn something by exploring these realms.

Consider that if you end up someplace strange, it might be for a reason. The universe might have a bit of knowledge to share with you, much as if you were having a nocturnal insight or encountering a dark omen. Explore these new experiences safe with the knowledge that you can return to your body at any moment if you feel frightened or confused.

You may even encounter astral beings. These could be manufactured beings, of the type you'll learn to make later on, or could be existing entities. The being could even be a dead person trying to reach out to you, or, believe it or not, just another living person out for an astral saunter.

Fear no one and no thing you encounter on the astral plane. They can't hurt you. Remember, if you feel anything negative about a particular encounter, simply will yourself back into your body or to another place, and it's taken care of.

In fact, rather than fear or flee those you encounter, try to communicate with them when you can. You never know what they might have to tell you.

And, if you get really daring, you can try planning an astral meeting with a friend once he or she masters the art of astral travel. Your imagination and experimentation are the only limits here, but you will be creating magick any time you try to learn or accomplish something on the astral plane. Remember, it's an interaction with the astral that makes all magick possible, and practicing such interaction directly, out of body, is never a wasted exercise.

Chapter Nine

Master of Mystique,
Mistress of Illusion

If you were to spend a few days moving with deliberation and giving real conscious attention to your actions, you would be creating magnetic vibes, so to speak. This subtle charging of your movements with emotional energy—as all concentration from a magickian raises some energy—would attract subconscious attention from others on an astral level. Said astral attention will manifest as conscious physical attention, too. This is the true power and mechanics of magnetism.

This is a fine thing to experiment with, but there will be some moments when you would like a specific boost to your magnetic presence — moments when you'd like to try active illusion to draw (or repel) others.

Read on and learn how to enhance the alluring energy around you.

Astral Nonprojection

We spent two chapters covering how to get out of your body, how to stay out of it, and how to control what occurs while you're out of it. But what if you become aware of your astral body and *don't* leave your physical one?

What we're about to delve into should not be tried until you've been successfully traveling astrally for at least a few weeks—preferably a few months. You be the judge of when you're ready, based on what you're about to read. Essentially, you can only try the following once you've achieved excellent control over your astral form.

Feeling Your Astral Body

The first couple of times you try this, do it seated. However, keep in mind that the goal is to be able to do this standing up.

Try to achieve some inner quiet.

Raise some emotional energy. Try to judge when you have reached approximately half of what you consider to be your peak, and maintain this level.

Immediately try to imagine the vibratory state that you feel when about to leave your body. Recreate this feeling as best as you can, drawing from the emotional energy that you raised to power the vibrations.

Continue in this manner for about thirty seconds. When you feel that you've almost got the feeling right, raise your emotional energy level to peak. Say:

I am in control of my astral form.

Relish the vibratory state that you should now be achieving with eyes open. Feel your astral form fully coinciding with your physical one, but make no attempt to leave your physical body (especially if you're standing up!).

Let the feeling fade after a few minutes. Do not try to banish it. Just let it run its course.

What's possible now? you might be wondering. To this I answer, "What isn't possible now?"

Advanced Illusion and Glamoury

A good amount of magnetism comes from working with energy, and mystique builds around the magnetic individual. As I hinted at earlier, having conscious awareness of your astral form will only enhance the alluring vibe around you, making your presence shine in the darkness.

From time to time, however, you will want to create something more specific about your person. Be that a subtle impression or something that may startle the attuned, it is achievable with advanced illusion and glamoury.

Here are some powerful ways to achieve illusions by relying on your newfound control of your astral form.

Making Them See

Firm up in your mind exactly what image you want others to think they sense or see when they look at you. Imagine exactly what this illusion would look like to those around you, if they could see it with their physical eyes. Whether you succeed at creating an impression or borderline hallucination will depend on both your effort and the perceptivity of the person you'll be trying to affect.

Create an affirmation of desire that describes this image of what you want others to sense or see. It can even be abstract, your statement, as long as you came up with a visual idea that is concrete. For example, a girl thinking, "I am alluring," might have a particular starlet in mind, or just a particular body enhancement. Either way, there's something definite in mind to flesh out the statement.

Achieve some inner quiet.

Raise about half your peak of emotional energy and repeat your affirmation of desire.

Make sure you fully imagine the vibratory state that puts you in touch with your astral form.

Now, try to see that awakening astral form taking the shape of whatever it is you want others to see.

When you think you can imagine this second skin and form, raise your emotional energy level to peak.

Say to yourself:

I am in control of my astral form. I am now (statement of desire).

Focus one last time on your visualized illusion, and let your vibratory awareness fade. However, the illusion should last for as long as you consciously think about it. That is, every few minutes you should imagine the visualization associated with your illusion and try to recall the vibratory state. Unless some dire need is at hand, I recommend you only try to keep an illusion going for about an hour or two, maximum. It's too draining and tiring to maintain for much longer.

By adding vibratory awareness, you can enhance most any rite that calls for emotional energy or astral manipulation. In time you might even try adding it to your true invocations or godform assumptions.

Rather than show you how to use awareness of your astral body in all types of rites you already know, though, I'll show here how to apply this awareness to a powerful and controversial occult topic:

Invisibility.

We've all heard that spells for such will result in people not noticing you, and so on. We've all likely found these spells to fail, too!

Let's see about making invisibility work for you. Whether you actually vanish or move unnoticed . . . I'll leave that up to you to make happen.

Making Them Not See

Perform a banishing of some type, being sure to create a circle/sphere of cleansed space (it should suffice to just imagine a sphere growing from within you until it creates a giant sphere around you). Spend a moment really feeling the border of the sphere you create—the barrier outside of where the night seems to solidify. Be sure to see the sphere as a dark one.

For a couple of minutes, gaze at a random point of the sphere in front of you, imagining that the sphere is becoming ever more solid.

Achieve some inner quiet and use a half-peak amount of emotional energy to become aware of your astral body.

Feel your aura magnetically calling to the perimeter of your dark circle, all while maintaining the beginnings of the vibratory state. With your attention split between your silver astral body and the surrounding dark sphere, say:

I will that the palpable darkness come to me.
I will that it cloak my aura and hide me from sight.

Begin to raise more emotional energy and visualize the dark sphere closing in on you. Try to time your peak so that it will hit when the sphere makes contact with your aura.

At the moment of dark connection, peak and say:

I am invisible.

See yourself as wearing the darkness like a thick powder that is stuck to your once-glowing astral form. Go and perform whatever task you wish to accomplish invisibly (again, the effect of the rite is up to your development and power levels). You will need to maintain at least a subtle awareness of the vibratory state and the "hugging" quality of the darkness touching your aura, so try to be quick about your unseen business.

To banish the effects, become increasingly aware of the vibratory state. Begin to sense that it is shaking the dark particles off your aura. Raise emotional energy with the intent to peak.

At your peak, see the remaining black particles blast off of you and into the darkness around. Say:

I am visible.
Yet come, dark cloak, whenever I call.

Again, use the awareness of your astral body to your advantage whenever you can in a rite. You should work on intuitively adding it to points in your rites when you feel you need an extra, tangible power boost.

Part Four

Fulfilling Dark Needs

Chapter Ten

Master of Thought

Too many beginners in the magickal arts perform rites without power. It's a more than subtle failing that occurs in the magickal world, and could be responsible for the "loss" of those who drop early from the mystical fold. In some ways, perhaps it's meant to occur, this loss. It could be a natural weeding out of those who think or wish that merely reciting a few lines will grant them their heart's desire. For if one is truly meant for magick, he or she will dig deeper and find the core principles that make magick work.

Manifestation—magick—is giving form to will and desire by working through the mental, astral, then physical planes. In the mental plane our thoughts, even accidental or abstract ones, and desires come into being. The astral plane lets our abstract thoughts begin to take shape on their own, to maybe one day manifest out of our control; but this astral plane is more importantly a realm where we can empower our strongest thoughts to magickally take shape soon. Finally, in the physical plane creation occurs, with our strongest formed thoughts taking tangible, noticeable form, and our abstract or accidental thoughts possibly appearing, too, even if we don't really want them to.

Note the important double nature of magickal creation: Things we actively wish for have a better chance of coming into being, but on some level, *everything* we think up has a shot at coming into being. Beware not just what you wish for, but what you didn't even realize you willed into being!

All thoughts have a chance of coalescing into thoughtforms on the astral plane. And most thoughtforms will then manifest physically, unless defeated by stronger thoughtforms. The ancients were wise to teach concentration, focus, and harmony to their magickal students. If the mind of a powerful Witch or magickian is a chaotic landscape, then chaos will manifest—literally—on the landscape of the world.

Chaos like this should be avoided.

By learning to add emphasis and extra power to the creation rites that we want to have work for us, we can make them work better, of course. However, we can also gain the important benefit of keeping lesser-powered accidental thoughts from manifesting.

Do you see? By training our subconscious to give extra precedence to the magick we do, we tell our mind to filter out random thoughts as being unworthy of any of our attention. Think of what you're about to learn as a way of bringing the concept of the inner quiet to the entire astral plane.

Only empower the thoughtforms that you truly desire bringing into being. This will help to keep your spiritual life uncluttered and filled with purpose. Unwanted thoughtforms can become distracting and even dangerous. Surround yourself by too many of them, and the resulting cloud will make it difficult for your true magickal desires to radiate and manifest in the universe.

Random Thoughts—How They Linger

An interesting thing about thoughtforms is that when they are consciously created, they are fired off into the astral plane to do their work. This is not the case with unintentionally created thoughtforms. Not properly programmed, accidental thoughtforms do their best, in a nonsentient way, to come to life.

Accidental thoughtforms can be one of three types, basically: negative, neutral, or positive. Each behaves differently, but, surprisingly, not one of them helps a magickian's operating and living environment. All contribute to the chaos discussed earlier.

Negative thoughtforms manifest when one has negative thoughts against the efforts of another. These ugly forms automatically seek out the potential victim of their energies. Envy someone's endeavors, for instance, and the thoughtform you unintentionally create will leech off those endeavors, hoping to destroy them. Hey, no one said the magickal nature of the universe was a fully "nice" thing.

Neutral thoughtforms are the ones that stick around. Random thoughts, of the type you try to clear away when achieving inner quiet, can develop their own strength. Anyone who claims the inability to concentrate, despite numerous efforts, is likely plagued by neutral thoughtforms. While they're not malignantly charged, these neutral thoughts add layers of "gray" to your aura and act as a blocking cloud of sorts. They leech off your own astral form and make it hard to send out the focused energies you wish to use in a rite.

Positive thoughtforms launch off on their own, kind of like negative ones, but do seek to do good. Unfortunately, even positive thoughtforms can have negative consequences. Remember how you're supposed to direct a rite toward results that are for the greater good? Well, unintentionally created positive thoughtforms don't know that! They'll go out and try to bring you the key to your dreams . . . while following the path of least resistance.

When you know there's something you really want, by all means do a proper rite to obtain it. Otherwise, you might accidentally set a thoughtform at work to bring the object of your desires to you in a very undesirable way.

You'll note that we're spending some space here talking about unwanted thoughts. This is because by controlling the unwanted forms, in even a passive way, you'll be actively strengthening every bit of magick you do from here on out. Really!

Disabling the Negative

It's easy for some so-called ascended master to say to us, "Banish all negative thoughts from your life."

Gee, is that all we need to do? Thanks for the advice, ascended one!

Let's be realistic here. Negative thoughts are normal and, in certain cases, healthy. Far better to dwell for a brief moment on how annoyed you are at something than to just pretend it doesn't matter and move on with pent-up rage.

You don't want to banish negative thoughts and attempt to become some kind of unfeeling drone. Not only would it be difficult to do, but it would backfire. I mean, build up too much steam, and just see what kind of thoughtform you'll one day unleash!

To keep negative thoughtforms from heading out on their not-so-merry ways, you have to acknowledge them—in a way, harbor them—for a few moments. Don't give power to them, understand, just examine them as real entities. You'll see in a moment that there's a way to actually use the power of negative thoughtforms against themselves.

As long as thoughtforms are under your mental scrutiny, they're not free to wreak countless disasters on the astral and maybe physical planes. So begin with a few moments of that scrutiny. This will actually have a calming effect on you. Instead of doing something silly and unfocused like counting to ten, really explore that next swelling of jealousy, anger, hate, or whatever. I know there are people cringing at these words, but please be honest with yourselves. Negative thoughts will well up on occasion. Acknowledge this fact, and acknowledge the thoughts when they appear. Then spend a minute exploring why you're feeling a particular way.

When you think you've got an idea why your happy or even ho-hum night was spoiled by whatever event is at hand, you are ready to disable the thought before it takes form . . . by giving it a form of your own.

Destroying a Negative Thought

Silently name the thought with a simple one- or two-word tag such as "jealousy."

See the thought floating in the air before you as a fragile sphere that is uneven and bumpy and colored a sickly brown. Make sure you are fully aware that this ugly form is "jealousy" or whatever you named it.

Pull on the very emotional energy that the thought created in you. You're not really drawing on this energy, but drawing it out of yourself.

Peak that energy and imagine the energy blasting out of your eyes to shatter the thoughtform.

Turn away slightly and tell yourself:

Master of my thoughts.

Immediately think of something that evokes in you the opposite sort of mood to the one you just experienced.

Carry on with the rest of your night, truly master of your thoughts.

That's an intelligent and realistic way to deal with the negative thoughts that plague us. Not only are you keeping troublesome thoughts from manifesting, but you're spending some extra time tensing that psychic muscle that lets you work with etheric matter—always a good thing.

Clearing the Neutral

Funny thing about neutral thoughts: If they're truly neutral, you don't care enough to notice them. Through your initial struggles to maintain inner quiet, however, you've likely seen just how many random thoughts can pass through your brain each minute. A good many of them are just insignificant enough to barely register—to remain background noise.

Yet even these unregistered, half-formed thoughts can gain power in time.

Should you repeatedly fall into the same trains of thought, the miniscule bits of energy given to these barely noticed thoughts will begin to accumulate. In time, even something as silly as "What time does that TV show begin tonight?" can turn into a cohesive bit of astral garbage. You might not remember pondering when *Charmed* was going to be on, but eventually a large chunk of etheric energy might float around your head with just such a query as its purpose for being.

What do these floating, neutral thoughtforms do? No real harm, but no real good, either. To use our current example, no, you won't spend all your time wondering when the show will be on. The thoughtform will, however, make it harder for you to concentrate on other things. This neutral thoughtform will, in time, begin to work with others of its kind to create what I like to call a "scatterbrain cloud" around you.

The more active control you take of your thoughts and their power, the less likely you are to create many of these distraction thoughtforms. Still, it's a good idea to get rid of the ones around you from time to time—maybe once a week while you're still working through all the techniques in these two nocturnal books. In time, you'll find that the need to do a cleaning only comes once every few months.

And you'll know when the buildup has gotten to the distraction point, believe me.

Clearing, Cleaning

Achieve some inner quiet (if it's difficult to do, you know you really need to perform this rite).

Raise some emotional energy—just enough to help you become aware of the vibratory state.

With eyes closed, try to see this awakened astral body of yours. Say:

> *Filter of the unseen, allow me to glimpse the unwanted within me.*

Using your imagination, begin to look for the ugly little thoughtforms that are stuck within your aura. Don't worry if it feels like you're just imagining that they're there.

Every time you find one of the little intruders, imagine it rising to the surface of your astral body so that it is almost completely free of this etheric boundary.

When you've done this "lifting" for each thoughtform, you will be left with a view of yourself analogous to someone wearing a suit of light bulbs. Your aura will have all these little globes stuck to its top layer.

Now, perform a banishing that involves you expanding a sphere from within you. However, as the sphere begins to grow out of you, see the little thoughtforms moving away from you, carried by the expanding aura sphere.

At the point when you conclude your banishing and finish the expansion of your aura sphere, see the little thoughtforms as moving away, carried by the momentum of the expanding circle. That is, you'll grow your sphere to a usual size (say, nine feet), but when it stops expanding the little thoughtforms attached to it will be jolted free and launched out into the night.

Say:

Master of my thoughts.

You are now free of distractions.

Reabsorbing the Positive

Nothing will bring chaos to your life more quickly than if you go shooting off your Witch power in every which direction. This applies even if you do so without knowing that you're doing it, too! Positive thoughtforms that are unintentionally formed might bring good to your life or to another's, or they might just mess everything up for everyone. I'm not being overdramatic here, just realistic. Again, recall the warning related to being wary of wishes. Thoughtforms can have a lot of power, and they can result in chaos when the universe takes the path of least resistance to manifest them.

It's wise, therefore, to not only try to control your thoughts, as we've said, but to also try to maintain control over the ones you didn't know you had sent out. Unlike examining when you're angry for some reason and then dispelling possible negative thoughtforms that could arise, the technique you're about to learn is more like the one for neutral thoughts. That is, you should do it from time to time, and know that in time you won't have to do it that often.

Unlike the neutral thoughtform technique, however, the one you're about to learn is designed to work with thoughtforms that have long since left your immediate aura. Accidental but positive thoughtforms "mean well," and try to get out and busy as soon as possible.

From time to time, you've got to try and bring these thoughts back home.

The Thoughtform Net

Achieve some inner quiet and perform a banishing.

Raise enough emotional energy to become aware of your astral body. Use some positive memories or thoughts to do so—make it really emotionally charged emotional energy.

Close your eyes and enjoy the harmonious feeling of an aura awakened by positive memories. Say:

Like attracts like, this and every night.
May the random good return to the matter from which it was born.

Imagine that a couple of silver, glowing thoughtforms are floating toward you. Feel them enter your aura and harmoniously vibrate within it. Feel their power being added to yours as they are reabsorbed.

Begin to raise the level of your emotional energy and see more thoughtforms coming. They will, in turn, raise your emotional energy even higher as you absorb them.

When you peak, try to absorb the last few silver spheres that appear. Say:

Master of my thoughts.

Allow the vibratory state to dissipate on its own—it should feel great!

Will you be able to do these thought-control techniques all the time? No, of course not, which is why I gave some realistic recommendations for frequency of repetition. But remember, the more you do these techniques, the more your subconscious will begin to appreciate how seriously you take your thoughts. And wonderful benefits will be the result.

Also, keep in mind that all of that active thinking you'll be giving to your thoughts will have a marvelous extra effect. In addition to clearing your thought fields and removing energy-draining or chaos-causing thoughtforms, you will also be training your mind to more quickly connect with astral thoughtforms. Any consciously created ones that you work with from now on will be far stronger!

Chapter Eleven

The Nocturnal Servant

With a little extra mental sharpening from the rites you learned in the last chapter, your abilities at manifesting desires will only grow. Time and practice is all it will take. Soon, most rites you perform will enable you to create dark miracles.

In your occult readings, you might have encountered mention of a type of manifestation that adds a new layer to the idea of a mystical miracle. Ever encounter tales of magickally created beings? Some rites can create a thoughtform that takes on a life of its own.

The legends of such beings have about them the feeling of just that—legend—coming often from exotic locales such as the mountains of Tibet. But they also have about them the ring of occult truth.

We won't go into retelling such stories here, be they from the Far East or from the Western world, such as the golem of Hebrew folklore or the homunculus of German occultism. Let's just point out the obvious parallel all these stories have to each other:

Thoughtforms have and can come to life, with a seeming intelligence all their own.

Caveat Conjuror

If you read any of the various retellings of a couple of the specific examples just mentioned—the golem and homunculus—you'll find that they have some things in common. On the positive side, they make it clear that while you need to have a lot of power to make a manufactured spirit of sorts, you get a decent return, too. Magickians throughout the ages have known that making a spirit can be a potent way to accomplish a lot of good, quickly.

On the negative side, however, comes the warning that such a spirit should not be allowed to wander the earth for eternity. Should such a thing happen, the spirit will gain a power of its own and bring new meaning to chaos. Basically, when a sentient thoughtform—sometimes called an *egregore* in ceremonial magick—is allowed to have an infinite lifespan, it begins to take liberties it has no right to take. This manufactured being, devoid of any conscience or true allegiance, begins to act on the primal impulses it was endowed with at its creation.

Let me explain with an example. Say you created a nocturnal servant or egregore to protect one of your coven members on a dangerous trip she had take soon. You might charge the being with the task of spooking away any who might mean your Witch harm. Innocent enough, really. You just want the nocturnal servant to provide the impression that your Witch is not worth the trouble of bothering, right?

Now let's say that your Witch goes on her trip and returns. You're so happy that she came back from the Middle East or wherever and is fine that you decide to let the little nocturnal servant keep at his job. He's not visible (most of the time) and doesn't seem to get in the way. What can it hurt? You like your Witch friend, and so what if an etheric being is protecting her from now on. That's a good thing, right?

No!

The nocturnal servant was created with just enough endowed intelligence to know how to protect your Witch on a particular trip. By specifying its job, you have allowed the spirit only enough freedom to act on anything that comes up during that trip. Once the trip has ended, the servant no longer has any real purpose for being. Without a clear set of parameters to operate within any longer, it will now try to adapt its purpose as it sees fit. Given time, it may begin to act on protective impulses whenever it feels your no-longer-traveling Witch is in danger. Maybe a boss plans on giving her too much work one night? Maybe someone had the nerve to cut in front of her in line outside the movie theater?

Are these really people who need to feel the wrath of an angry spirit?

And that wrath itself may grow as the motives driving the spirit evolve. Again, this is all about manifestation. The nocturnal servant will become more real with time, just like any thoughtform. As a result, it will develop more real, if irrational, thought processes, as well as more real powers with which to act on its impulses. What started as a simple servant meant to subtly scare off any who mean harm to the Witch could end up a demonic being bent on physically destroying anyone who so much as frowns in the Witch's direction!

Granted, this sort of thing doesn't happen all the time, but egregores or spirit servants are not made all the time, either . . . at least not consciously. For all we know, children do it accidentally. I've even met people whose imaginary friends told them real, verifiable facts in childhood! And sometimes such "friends" become all too physical, also. Poltergeists have long been tied to adolescent children who might be exhibiting latent psychic ability. Maybe these children really just had imaginary friends to which they gave too much power.

As the practice of creating a servant is an advanced one, it comes with the advanced responsibility of assigning a finite lifespan. Come up with a set job for the being to accomplish, and make sure this job can be accomplished within a moon cycle or two. Do not, under any circumstances, allow a nocturnal servant to live any longer than that. At the end of the predetermined time period, perform the ritual destruction rite you will learn here.

And keep in mind: Should you choose to ignore this rule, the person most likely to be harmed by your creation is you! It's no accident that most folklore and even movies about manufactured "monsters" contain a scene where the magickian or good doctor responsible for the being comes to a horrible demise. Nocturnal servants, like any other egregore, would logically, in time, seek to eliminate the one person who can stop their power trip or attempts at freedom.

None of these warnings are meant to scare you away from the practice—just to make you undergo it responsibly. Creating a nocturnal servant is foolproof—as with any properly performed magick—as long as you follow a few simple rules. Just like any rite, creating a nocturnal servant should be done with the greater good in mind. This means also assigning a night on which your nocturnal servant will cease to exist.

Benefits Abound

We'll get right to the "how" of making nocturnal servants in a moment, but must now take advantage of the attention-grabbing nature of subheads to point out how positive the practice can be for you. Unlike thoughtforms, which are best designed for one specific goal that the universe seeks the path of least resistance to manifest, a nocturnal servant can be created to repeatedly accomplish a type of goal for a set period of time. You'll find some things just need repeated doing.

The possibilities are endless, but a couple more examples should help you figure out why you'd choose to manufacture a servant rather than just a thoughtform.

Looking to bring love into your life? Use a thoughtform to attract someone with the general qualities you'd like him or her to possess. Looking to actively keep away those who might not be so ideal while you are undergoing your search? Use a servant to subtly deter those who possess certain traits you've identified as being highly undesirable (sneaky, married, into disco, whatever).

Hunting for a job? A thoughtform can bring the right one to you. But what if you get nervous in job interviews? It might be tough to do a spell before every appointment you get. Rather, you can create a servant to help bend probabilities at the meetings you go to and swing things in your favor. Little tasks this being does can help, such as ensure things are running smoothly a few minutes before you arrive, and maybe distract your interviewer from awkward statements your nerves might have you make.

Have a special piece of property you'd like to keep safe? A protective spell or thoughtform might expire the first time it deterred someone from taking this property. A nocturnal servant, however, could act as a sentry for a month or two, repeatedly stepping in when necessary. I always have one of these guys in my library, although I repeatedly make new ones for the task as old ones are destroyed.

I could go on, but I think you might be getting the idea by now. Nocturnal servants can continually act on a specific desire of yours, approaching it with different tactics as circumstances dictate. Unlike thoughtforms, which settle for the path of least resistance to get their work done, a nocturnal servant has the time and limited intelligence necessary to repeatedly work toward achieving your long-term goals.

The Sentient Form

The form your nocturnal servant takes is up to you. Some may feel comfortable giving the being the shape of a sphere, as they would with a standard thoughtform. I prefer to make servants that are anthropomorphic or humanoid, and somewhat targeted to the work at hand. It's natural to imagine a human-like being working on a goal, and giving it traits to accomplish that goal only helps.

For example, if you need help getting a better job, you might create a servant that almost resembles a lawyer—a being that resonates a sense of success in the business world. Unless you're trying to find, say, a better tattoo parlor to work for, in which case you might want a very different-looking servant helping you out.

The form you choose for the servant can have some preternatural elements. For instance, you might find it helpful to give a phantom protector some claws or fangs if it helps your feeling of security. Just be careful not to ask the thing to use such protective gear to do any flesh shredding! The purpose of providing symbolic extras such as these is to help make the thing more "visually" enabled to perform its job. If someone senses claws or fangs on any level, that person will have an uncomfortable feeling and naturally shy away. He or she won't know why, but will be more inclined to stay out of the path of your protector . . . and you!

In any case, you'd have to spend a major amount of energy trying to make a being tangible enough to cause any harm with something like claws or fangs. And even if you did succeed, the karmic consequences of the violent being's actions would be all yours.

Actually, keep that in mind in general: Your servant's actions are, for all the universe knows, your actions. Use this being for evil, and evil will come to you.

With the form in mind, you're just about ready to create a servant. Again, this being will be etheric. Creating a solid one might take years of repeated experimentation—or much less time with the help of the right group of people. A finely tuned coven might be able to combine its efforts toward such a solid aim, literally, as long as the coven is finely tuned. Creating a physical servant is not something to try if a coven is beginning to lose its cohesiveness.

The rite for creating a servant is given for a single person, but can easily be modified for a group. Different people can take part in casting the circle, and then everyone can focus energy on the outcome at the appropriate spot. However, there is no modification needed to the rite to make it more suitable for creating a physical servant. The only thing that determines the physical nature of the servant you end up with is the amount of energy that goes into its creation.

The Preparations

You will need to do more than just imagine the form of your nocturnal servant clearly. You must make a physical housing for this thing to rest in when it's not actively working. The physical representation won't need to be perfect—no real sculpting skills are necessary. As long as the statue generally reminds you of the being you imagined, it will serve its purpose. However, the statue will need to be "destroyable," so you will want to make it from nonhardening modeling clay. If you can find it, obtain black clay; if none is available, try mixing some black ink into white or beige clay. You'll need to fold and mash the clay, and apply more ink as needed. This works pretty well and creates a decidedly night-like color.

Do not use clay of another color, even if you feel it applies to the task the servant will be performing. You'll see why black clay is necessary in a moment.

Form the clay into a general form of the being that you imagine. Try to give it physical traits that get across its reason for being. Maybe big hands for a servant intended to gather things? Maybe four legs for something that you want to be quick moving? You decide on what form makes the most sense, see it clearly in your mind, and do your best to recreate the form in clay. The servant's form can be as fantastic, mythical, or mundane as you wish it to look.

Make the figure at least six inches tall, although you can make it larger if you wish to be able to add more detail. When deciding on size, however, make sure you'll have a place to hide the figure when you're done. Also, be sure you can part with this large amount of nonhardening clay for good. You will not be able to reuse it.

Next comes the need to write your intent in spell form. This requires coming up with a name for your servant. Try to make it something that doesn't remind you of anything else. Don't pick a character from a favorite novel, for instance. You want the name, simple or extravagant as it may be, to make you think only of your servant. If you're really stuck, take a foreign language dictionary and switch a letter or two around from the first word you find. It will sound exotic, at the very least, and will fuel your magickal sense of wonder.

Write your spell as a command for the servant to do what you ask. Add a reference to whatever deity you will be invoking for help. Obviously, you will want to pick a deity that is somehow related to the task at hand. Also, add a reminder of how long this being will be allowed to live. Make it clear in your spell/command, too, that you have created a servant who will harm none while carrying out its tasks. Don't worry about the words for actually creating the servant, though, as those are given in the rite.

Something like this will work:

Daseni, having been brought to life by my will and the will of
(name of the God or Goddess), I now command you.
Guide me, Daseni, to the best job opportunities that I seek.
Whenever you venture out from this clay form, may your efforts also
be dedicated to smoothing my path for each interview you help me obtain.
Daseni, you have until the next Full Moon to perform these tasks.
And you will carry out your tasks with harm to none, for the greater good.
So mote it be.

Remember, the spell is a form of command. It must be specific, even if it ends up being somewhat long.

Note that this servant was given a lifespan of one moon cycle. While a moon cycle or two is a practical maximum, the minimum is up to you. If a being is supposed to have a very moon-phase-like task, such as banishing, then you might want to let it live only long enough to follow the particular phase. For example, create a spirit meant for banishing on the Full Moon and let it live until the New Moon, when its powers would peak anyway. However, if a servant is needed to assist in completing a one-night task, then its lifespan is pretty obvious.

Again, never let a servant live beyond the completion of its task. I can't stress this enough.

Granting Life

You will need to set up your altar for a normal circle casting. Have present whatever you need to invoke the God or Goddess of choice. Your invocation should mention that you seek help of the God or Goddess in bringing life to clay, but the rest of the invocation can be just as you would normally write one (for instance, mention the traits of the deity you are seeking, your desire, and how you seek help achieving it). Note that for a rite of this intensity, you are best off performing a true invocation or godform assumption if you know how to do so. You'll need the extra power. Another way of calling up some extra magickal juice, so to speak, would be to adapt the rite to group work.

Also on the altar should be your spell of commanding, the clay figure, and a toothpick. Burn the heaviest incense you can find—a gum resin like mastic is ideal.

The Nocturnal Servant Rite
Cast a magick circle.

Invoke the God/dess, remembering to specify why you want this deity's help in creating a servant to do a particular task.

Pick up the clay form with your receiving hand and walk clockwise to the eastern edge of your circle.

Reach straight out to touch the head of the form to the edge of your circle. Feel that some of the dark energy present at the boundary is pulling into the figure.

Begin to walk clockwise, holding the head of the figure to the circle edge and drawing in the dark energy. Say:

Form of clay, the dark ether fills you with the potential for life.

Feel some of the energy making it through the form and into you. Repeat your circumambulation two more times. Each time, let the feeling of present energy build. Also each time around, increase speed to react to the growing energy. By the time you return to the east edge of the circle the last time the clay figure should almost be throbbing.

Stop suddenly at the east. Pull the figure away from the circle edge, bringing it right in front of your face. Say (almost shout) with a commanding tone:

You will live, this night!

Move clockwise around your altar to return to your spot with the altar before you. Continue to hold the clay figure in your receiving hand.

Pick up the toothpick with your projecting hand and hold it in the incense smoke. Begin to raise a little emotional energy (about one-third of your peak) and feel this moving up your projecting arm and into the toothpick. See the little piece of wood glowing etherically.

Take the toothpick from the smoke and raise a little more energy to about the halfway level. Feel and see this practically igniting the end of the toothpick. Bring this glowing point of wood to the approximate heart spot of the figure's chest.

Try to maintain your energy level as you write the name of the being in the chest of the figure. See the glowing tip not only carve through the clay, but sizzle it and leave a glow behind.

With the name blazing on the figure, drop the toothpick onto the altar. Shift your gaze from the glowing name to the nocturnal portal. Try to see the letters of the name floating there while allowing your skrying vision to awaken.

Now comes the part that requires the most concentration. Allow your emotional energy level to slowly rise as you see the letters morphing in the nocturnal portal. See their glowing light turning into a silver mist. As your energy approaches near peak, see the mist form into the shape of the nocturnal servant (the true, detailed shape with features—not the representation you ended up with in the clay).

When you're almost at the peak point and can see the servant clearly, "pull" this vision from the portal with your eyes. See the servant's astral body, which you just created, leap from the portal and into the clay figure.

Hit full peak and place your projecting hand (the one you write with) over the figure. Feel yourself forcing energy into the thing.

Read or recite your spell, commanding the being.

Pull your projecting hand away and place the figure on the altar. Imagine the living form you created cohabiting the clay form before you. Say:

Nocturnal Servant, (name),
I command you to leave this clay form only when you need to perform
one of your assigned tasks.
Whenever you are not zealously carrying out my will, you will return to this form.
And on (the deadline), you will return to this form before nightfall.

Close your circle.

Thank the God/dess for being with you.

Put the nocturnal servant's form in a place where no one else will come into contact with it. Store the paper on which you wrote the command spell in the same place.

The servant will now, as it needs to, etherically fly out into the world to carry out its assigned tasks. From time to time you might sense it— even see it. Do not let it alarm you. Remember, you are its maker. It is merely doing what you wish it to, and in no way can it harm you . . . as long as you follow through with what comes next. . . .

Bringing Death

When the deadline for the nocturnal servant's lifespan arrives, you must be sure to put an end to the being's existence. Do not put it off for even one night, as that goes against the thoughtform you created, and may put the servant out of your immediate control.

Nocturnal servants are powerful magickal tools and can bring much good into your life. Just don't try to test what happens when you let such a powerful force slip out of your immediate control!

With that warning repeated, let's move on to the process of bringing death to your created lifeform.

Your altar will need to be set up to invoke the same deity you did on the night of the servant's creation. Modify your invocation to reflect that you now want this deity's help in destroying the servant.

Place the clay figure on the altar, along with the original command spell used in the creation. You will also need a suitable container for burning paper—either an ashtray or a little cauldron will work just fine.

Dismissing the Servant

Cast a magick circle.

Invoke the same deity you called to help you create the servant.

Lift up the figure with your projecting hand and try to see the nocturnal servant lurking within. Establish imaginary eye contact with the being. Say:

> *In the name of the God/dess (invoked deity),*
> *I thank you for your service, (servant name).*
> *For your service which has now ended.*
> *I now release your energy to the dark ether.*

Wipe and press at the part of the figure where the name was written so that you smudge it out of existence. See a phantom version of the name linger in glowing silver letters for a moment, then fade away after the physical lines are already gone from appearance.

Walk counterclockwise to the east edge of your circle. Gaze at the servant's astral body one last time, seeing that its features are now indistinct. Only a general astral haze of silver energy inhabits the clay.

Touch the head of the figure to the edge of the circle and feel the energy from the clay moving back to the darkness outside.

Move around the circle counterclockwise at a brisk pace, keeping the figure's head in contact with the perimeter. This time, however, you will *slow down* a little with each circumambulation.

Before you complete your third and final circumambulation, you should be moving at an almost creeping pace. You should feel the last of the energy leave the figure when you come to the east the last time.

Break the figure in half and, reverently, walk counterclockwise to the west edge of the circle. Say:

> *I send you, creature of clay, to the night that has drained you.*
> *I send you to the gate of death.*

Toss the two pieces of the figure out of the circle toward the west.

Pivot clockwise and move to your standard position with the altar before you.

Pick up the original spell and light it with an altar candle. Say:

> *The effects of the servant's work maintain their permanence.*
> *It is done.*

Drop the burning paper into your fireproof container of choice.

Thank the deity for helping you.

Close the circle.

After you have your drink and treat, recover the pieces of the clay figure. Squeeze them so that they are unrecognizable globs of clay. Bury these pieces somewhere in your yard where they are not likely to be disturbed.

Try to never use the same name for a servant again. You can keep a record if this helps.

Chapter Twelve

Banishing, Exorcising . . .
with Darkness

One of the so-called darkest aspects of Sumerian magick was the system's focus on exorcism. Many of the negative experiences that befell the Sumerians, from poor health to legal disputes, were blamed on the presence of demons. By exorcising said demons, a magickian could make things better for the besieged Sumerian. In fact, most mages were even called exorcists, to reflect the nature of their predominant tasks.

Successful tasks, I might add. There was no doubt in the minds of citizens of the advanced Mesopotamian civilization that the exorcists were effective. Along with mathematics, engineering, agriculture, and other sciences that the Sumerians began to master, the knowledge of the existence of magick and demons was just as objective and factual.

Were there really thousands of demons roaming the desert, looking to attack those in the Fertile Crescent? Anything's possible, I suppose, but there might be another explanation. What if the exorcists were mostly banishing negative thoughtforms?

Facing or Making Demons?

In *Summoning Spirits: The Art of Magical Evocation* I show readers how to summon all manner of intelligences or entities to visible appearance, demons included. Interestingly, though, even after having seen more demons than all the horror movies combined have ever portrayed onscreen, I still can't be sure that these things always exist independent of us.

Are these beings just thoughtforms that we give reality to—much like a nocturnal servant—or are they really out there waiting for us to call or otherwise run into them? It might be a bit of both, actually.

There's a very good chance that the entities described in the ancient grimoires and the demons encountered by the Sumerians are all collective thoughtforms. Each named by some magickian or writer of legends, these beings would have been ready to accept both energy and form from the masses to come to life at an appropriately sinister time. Think about it and consider an example.

Let's say some Sumerian scribe came up with the idea of something called Pazuzu—a demon he blamed for pestilence (always lots of pestilence in ancient times, ever notice?). This scribe would put an interesting description of this demon down on a clay tablet for others to read and think about, and he'd then go on to carry out some other court- or priesthood-appointed task. Meanwhile, Pazuzu would begin to take on reality in the minds of the citizens who either read the tablet or heard about the demon at the temples. Even children would hear of him, and might have a hard time sleeping if they felt a strange wind at night that could be the beating of Pazuzu's wings.

And what would happen the next time pesky pestilence turned up? Why, the local priest or exorcist would consult the religious lore and find that he might know just who is up to no good. A banishing or exorcism of Pazuzu would have to be done at the perceived epicenter of the plague at hand.

Something amazing would occur at this exorcism, too. Pazuzu, the horrid demon, might actually make an appearance. Some citizens, children included, and definitely the exorcist would get a sense of the winged thing with rotting privates appearing during the rite. And with the rite ended and Pazuzu banished for at least a while (heh, heh) the pestilence would pass for a while, as well. Everyone would hail the exorcist, and life in Sumer would go on.

What really occurred in such an ancient exorcism? Assuming that Pazuzu was actually invented by some scribe, and that he didn't just so happen to let us mere mortals know his name, we can try to explain this demon's objective reality in the following way.

Pazuzu attained a general form from the scribe's descriptive prose. People around town then began hearing about, discussing, and imagining this thing, maybe for several years. Finally, when pestilence appeared again, the locals immediately attached all their belief in Pazuzu to the phenomenon, giving the plague a supernatural scapegoat. As a thoughtform, Pazuzu already had power and form by this time, kind of like your nocturnal servant while it is in the portal waiting to be dragged into the clay figure. Remember, all thoughtforms manifest eventually. Pazuzu could very well have brought about a plague on his own. But even if the demon didn't directly cause whatever befell the Sumerians, their blaming him as a group and attaching him to the scene of the crime, so to speak, would drag Pazuzu out of purely astral existence and into a temporary physical manifestation.

That's an important thing to note. Demons have been created by humans for millennia, and we continue to create them, or at least negative thoughtforms, to this day. But whether demons are actually responsible for bringing us woe on their own, or whether we just attach them to a woe (as etheric scapegoats), doesn't matter. Once a demon is magickally blamed for something, the weight of said crime is definitely on his or her shoulders. Interesting, huh?

It also happens that, once a demon becomes identified as the cause for a problem, banishing the demon acts as a sympathetic magick rite. Just as you can make a voodoo doll and stab away an illness, you can banish a demon to sympathetically banish some physical woe. It doesn't matter if poor old Pazuzu really did kill plants or form boils on the Sumerians. He took the blame, repeatedly, and each time this phantom fall guy was sent back to his corner of the astral plane, the Sumerians were left with a state of peace.

Of course, each time Pazuzu was banished, he also became stronger and more real, drawing from the renewed belief in the people of the time. Think of demon vanquishing as a self-propagating business.

What can we learn from this glimpse of how demonic scapegoating works? For one, if you're going to blame some negative thought-form for what's happening in your life, you're best off not trying to name it! That will only create a "demon" of sorts that's worthy of a return appearance. Should a demon somehow make itself known to you by name, well then you have no choice but to acknowledge it and make the most of the situation by banishing it. But understand that this is rare. Don't think you're going to venture out in the world encountering infernal fiends everywhere you look. The belief in demons is not so widespread anymore, and as a result there's less energy that the "established" ones can use to make a visible or noticeable appearance.

Negative thoughtforms, however, abound. Remember, most people don't know how to get rid of their own negative thoughtforms, as you learned to do in this book. Now we'll move into how you can do some good by getting rid of thoughtforms for others, too.

Exorcism

Right off, I should point out that we will not be dealing with full-on demonic possession in this book. Whether you believe the phenomenon is related to demons or some psychological or biological condition, the fact that the phenomenon and its related symptoms exist is irrefutable. When a person is fully possessed, speaking in tongues and hurling people around a room as if they were stuffed animals, this person needs very special care. I've done a few exorcisms and have found that the most important consideration is the individual's religion. If he or she is very strictly Catholic, for instance, sometimes only the drama of having a priest perform an exorcism will help. However, it is also possible to use enough symbolism from a person's religion to make the rite work for a nonpriest as well. Interestingly, much as psychodrama helps a magickian or Witch carry out a ritual, it also helps a possessed person let the ritual get through to him or her.

Full-on possession that falls in the Hollywood range of pea-soup spitting and levitation is rare. To delve into that requires an entire book on the subject of demons and their effects on the living.

For now, though, what you're about to learn can be used to banish negativity and demonic-like presences from places or people.

In the case of a place in need of such a cleansing, the people living there would experience anything from "bad vibes" and odd temperature changes to the witnessing of poltergeist phenomena. More disturbing would be the intense negativity that would color every action and thought of those in the room.

When a person is besieged by demons, he or she might see the negative beings in dreams or while trying to sleep. People besieged in such a way may seem as if their actions are subtly not their own—that they are acting on impulses seeming to come from elsewhere. When such people have been helped mystically, they always comment on how, in hindsight, they remember the time they spent under the influence almost as if they had been wearing sunglasses and cotton in their ears. Memories of the time are literally dim.

Should you encounter someone seeking your help because they sense intense negativity, you can feel assured that no harm can come from you doing a rite to banish negativity. Even if the phenomena occurring to these people were only stress-related or some such, then the process of scapegoating to some nameless negative thoughtform can't hurt; as sympathetic magick, it can only help. And if the person already believes that there's something sinister at play, convincing him or her otherwise might be difficult anyway. Better to help in the "expected" way by banishing evil, then let the person move on with life.

Just be careful not to let those seeking your help get carried away with their paranoia. Do not introduce a word like "demon" if they're only talking about negativity. And if they bring up demons, do try to tell them that sometimes negative thoughtforms are mistaken for demons. No need to overwhelm people with the true explanation that all demons are most likely just negative thoughtforms, anyway. Let them know of the possible explanation of demons and tell them that what you are about to do will help.

Note that the banishing is not given in the form of a full circle casting. To have such a requirement would mean that you could only help Witches or those quite friendly to Pagan ways. The following is a ritual that pulls purely on your power and abilities—and a little silent Divine help.

No tools are needed. Only a simple preparation, depending on whether you're doing the rite for a person or place.

If a person is affected by perceived negative beings, seat him or her to the east of the room, facing west. You will need to be about five feet away, and ensure thereby that there is a nine-foot space to create a circle, with the person just outside.

If it is a room that is affected, make sure to perform this rite in the center of the room, clearing space for a nine-foot-wide circle if need be.

Either way, whether doing the rite for a person or room, make sure that there is also about a foot or two worth of clear space to the west of your circle. You'll soon see why this is necessary.

Banishing Negativity

Stand at the center of the nine-foot circle area that you've chosen. If this rite is being performed for a person, ask him or her to remain seated. Should restraint of said person be required, then this ritual might not be strong enough to work, and a full exorcism would be necessary (again, out of the scope of this book).

Close your eyes and imagine that you are standing between two energy forms: one below, one above. The one below you is a black sphere that represents the astral body of the earth. Focus on how solid that one is for a moment before turning your attention upward.

Above you is a glowing silver maelstrom, shining in the darkness. Much like the whirlpool of cosmic light, this spiral is like a cone, with its arms connected at a luminous point well above you. The other ends of these trailing streams of light spread around you and sink into the ground below, just within the nine-foot space you've chosen. They slowly rotate clockwise, these arms, burning and purifying the area you've chosen to cleanse.

Now, see all the arms slowly begin closing in toward you at the same time. Say:

> *The whole of Divine fire approaches.*
> *May I be a worthy vessel.*

When only a foot away from you, the trailing arms should begin to straighten themselves out, becoming almost like a tight cage of crackling energy surrounding you. Feel the energy, but don't fear it. It only burns away evil.

Continue to see the beams approaching. Let them enter your skin as a blazing sheath of silver light, and feel them coalesce into a solid beam that passes through the center of you, of your spine, connecting above to below.

Relish the ecstasy for a moment.

With eyes still closed, look up and note that above you now the maelstrom has resolved itself into a massive silver sphere. Too large to fully comprehend, the sphere has too much energy to be contained in the beam passing through your core. See how much extra energy is crackling around the point where the beam emerges from the sphere.

Reach your arms straight up and say:

> *Divine fire awaits my use.*

Feel the crackling, excess energy touching your fingertips. You will be pulling this extra energy into you.

Take a deep breath to start the influx. Slowly lower your arms, feeling yourself pulling the excess energy in through your head. On this first breath, stop at about shoulder level (with arms pointing straight out at your sides). Exhale and feel the energy that is pulsing in your head, neck, and shoulders increase in intensity, swirling around the center beam of light within you.

Breathe in again, this time while lowering your arms to 45-degree angles and bringing the energy to your hips. Exhale, letting the energy pulse all the way down as far as your hips—again, freely coursing around the middle beam.

Take a third breath, lowering your arms to your sides and imagining the energy moving down to your feet. Exhale, seeing and feeling all the energy in your body coursing around the center beam of silver. You should feel as energized now as you ever have, if not more. Sense how you are, in fact, overflowing with energy.

Say:

> *Unable to contain the fire of the Gods, I send it out about me.*
> *May the fire purify.*

Open your eyes and enjoy for a moment your altered state of awareness. Give in to any egotistical sensation you get at this point. At this stage of the rite, you should *know* that you are as powerful as you feel.

Take a deep breath, feeling (almost impossibly) that even more energy is coursing down the center beam. Exhale, allowing the coursing silver lightning to expand out of you. By the time this first exhalation is complete, there should be a crackling, silver oval of lightning surrounding you, reaching out about a foot in every direction, including the ground below you. Really visualize this filled shape, with all its countless sparks and trails of silver swirling within. It has a definite perimeter, but not a smooth one. It is jagged and fiery. You are at the center of the chaotic energy oval, and at your center still is the bright silver beam.

On your next inhalation, feel more energy pouring down into you from above and spreading out into the jagged oval. Feel the energy's intensity and how it's barely containable in the field around you. Exhale, letting the oval expand about three more feet in every direction. See how it is now a six-foot-wide energy sphere, although it is still jagged and sparking at its perimeter.

Take another deep breath, bringing down enough energy to squeeze against the perimeter of the expanded sphere. When you exhale this time, the crackling nova of energy will expand to about nine feet wide. If you are doing this rite for a person, see the jagged edge just barely missing his or her legs.

Now come the few tricky steps, which happen to be amazingly effective.

Inhale deeply, without trying to bring down more energy, and hold this breath.

Take a step backward, suddenly, moving right out of the central energy beam's path!

Exhale, but don't allow yourself to adjust to the disorientation you feel. You've just created an energy imbalance in the crackling sphere and must take advantage of it.

Breathing normally, continue to move backward, to the west, until you walk right out of your energy sphere. Doing so can't hurt you, despite how odd it will feel to exit.

Spread your arms as if to hug the sphere. Say:

> *And this holy fire still bends to my will.*
> *Coalesce before me, for we stand ready to destroy present evil.*

Breathe in, raising about one-fourth of your peak level of emotional energy. Exhale, closing your arms slightly and willing the energy ball to shrink to about a six-foot sphere again. Take a step forward as you do so. After the sphere shrinks, feel how hot and pulsing it is—how it doesn't really "want" to be this small, for it hasn't lost any of its internal energy in the size change.

Take another deep breath, raising your emotional energy level to about halfway. As you exhale, step forward and close your arms a little more, willing the jagged sphere to shrink to about three feet wide. You should now be able to hold the energy sphere in your two hands, although it will be slightly uncomfortable. The pressure emanating from the sphere is immense. From this distance you can make out that the center energy beam is still there, inside the sphere.

Breathe deeply, raising about three-fourths of your peak energy level. Exhale, willing the sphere to close to a seemingly impossible eight- or nine-inch sphere of silver lightning. Step forward and close your hands to about a foot apart, noting how you can barely touch the crackling energy ball. It is suspended in air on the axis of the center energy beam.

After a few seconds of maintaining your own energy level with normal breathing, say:

The fire is released to me.

See the energy beam disappear, leaving the energy sphere suspended in air. Immediately take a deep breath to peak your energy level, and yell as loud as you can:

I banish evil!

Throw the energy sphere, using only your projecting hand. The direction depends on the rite's purpose.

If you are cleansing a room, throw the sphere straight down to the floor. See and feel it explode on impact, sending silver lightning in a burst toward every inch of the room. Feel the energy rush through you as it passes.

If you are cleansing a person, throw the energy sphere right at him or her. See the sphere crackle on impact, some of it passing straight through, some of it sparking around his or her torso. Note with your astral senses (which will be temporarily heightened at this point) if any ugly thoughtforms seem to burn away.

Drop to the ground and try to regain normal breathing. Ground yourself for a few moments before either leaving the room or discussing the rite with the person for whom you just performed it—that is, the person who should be feeling a lot better right about now.

Part Five

Nocturnicon

Chapter Thirteen

Quick, Powerful Rites

From this page forth, this gothic grimoire becomes a pure codex of nocturnal rites—a Nocturnicon, if you will. The topics that required a fair amount of explanation were found in earlier pages. This Nocturnicon is a gathering of things to which you can apply your knowledge at any stage in your development, and from which you can derive immediate (or at least pretty quick) benefit.

In this particular chapter, we'll be focusing on specific dark rites that nightkind may find useful. By explaining why I found one of them in particular useful, I have revealed a painful secret about my past, but I thought it could only help. Overcoming obstacles is one of the greatest things that magick can help us do, and I'm proud of my victories, small and large, and hope they'll help some of you get past some of your own mystical and physical hurdles.

The rites found here are for immediate use, of course, but they can also be examined as examples of what you can do when you apply the basics of magick to noticeably dark goals. Maybe the rites will even inspire you to try some different things with your spell creating and casting. I hope so. Magick should never get boring!

The disclaimer at the beginning of this book applies mostly to the rites you're about to explore in this chapter. Proceed with caution and only if you're comfortable with working magick to the extreme. Make sure you're willing to put your literal blood into a rite if necessary!

Some may find the subject matter of these rites a bit too dark and question my choices—particularly after reading the Spells to Send Things Away section. To such critics I say, "Have you been reading so far?"

We nightkind tend to find ourselves in different sorts of situations than true diurnal or light folks. That's just the way it is, and I see nothing wrong with writing about magick that suits our needs.

Also note that I won't be recommending whether you do a banishing or full magick circle, or a simple or true invocation. Depending on how much time you have, and what you feel capable of pulling off at a given moment, the preparations will have to be up to you. In fact, in only one case will I even be recommending a particular deity for you to call upon.

Consider each of these rites to be the magick you do after you set up whatever preliminaries you wish.

Spells to Bring Things to You

Ideally, when the moon is increasing, you want to do magick to bring into your life things, energies, people, whatever. However, in a pinch, these spells will work whenever you have the need for what they promise.

Increase Concentration During the Day

Whether you're finding it hard to get through class or work, a little magickal boost can help. We all know that it would be better to be sleeping and dreaming during the day, awaiting sweet night. But it doesn't always work out that way, and mundane needs require us to often be sharp when the sun's light all but stings.

Here's how to bring some night to your day.

Begin drawing a small, penny-sized, solid black circle on the center of a piece of blank white paper. Use the messiest, inkiest pen you can find. The more globs of black ink that normally form on the tip of the pen, the better it will be for this rite.

Begin to raise some emotional energy as you create the solid circle, and gradually begin to expand the circle's size with intense, outwardly spiraling, clockwise pen strokes (but try to make the circle look as solid as possible as it grows). Feel your emotional energy rising as the circle expands.

When the circle takes up about half the diameter of the paper (when one-quarter of the width of the paper is blank to either side) begin chanting the following, even if only to yourself:

Sphere of night, my current light.

Repeat this as the circle continues to grow, and you continue raising emotional energy.

Watch for the first time that your pen slips off the paper because of your speed and intensity, and because of the size of the circle. Get ready to peak and say the chant one last time.

Peak the very next time that your pen slips off the edge of the paper, repeat the chant, and toss your pen to the side.

Immediately pick up the paper and rip it in half. See and feel, with all your pent-up emotional intensity, that a black, etheric sphere has been launched or freed from the paper and sent into the air above you.

Observe the sphere floating there, casting what almost looks like a shadow upon you. This dark light, or absence of light, really, is pure, nocturnal ether. Say:

Be my clarifying light until you merge with night.

From time to time, take a quick, appreciative peek at the sphere. You'll find that you won't need to do so often, however, as your concentration on whatever diurnal task is before you will now be sharpened.

Draw a Date into Your Immediate Future

Admit it—not even the hippest club will yield romance every time. We all have our standards, be they physical, emotional, spiritual, or a combination—and you'll need a combination for any sort of longevity, obviously. But not every date needs to be about longevity, and on any given night it's okay to look for only . . . well, for whatever it is you're looking for on that night.

Here's a way to bring your general thoughts and desires to fruition, without tempting the wrath of karma through attempted mind control.

Consider if you want your date to bring you just one or more of the following three needs: physical, emotional, or spiritual companionship. For each type of need you determine is present, pick a disposable physical symbol. Want to find someone who is pale? Grab a piece of chalk. Want to meet someone who won't hurt you? Find an *empty* box of Kleenex. Want a date who is also into the occult? Draw a favorite occult symbol on a piece of paper.

In no way should you be trying to attract a particular person with this rite. However, it is okay to use a combination of that person's traits that you admire. As it's only one physical, emotional, and spiritual trait you're linking to, at most, there's no way you can be guilty of targeting a specific individual. And, if the universe just so happens to find you *two* to be a perfect match, well. . . .

Anyway, take your disposable symbols to wherever you can be alone in the dark, and light the biggest fire that's safely possible. A big cauldron or reasonably sized tin can will do, as will a fireplace or a charcoal barbecue. With the exception of the fireplace, I suggest you do this rite outside. Lighting a big fire indoors will only bring you a dream date if he or she also happens to be a firefighter!

Use your best judgment to decide what combination of wood, coal, or other fuel to use, depending on where this fire will be. A simple, ready-to-burn, store-bought log will work indoors, and self-lighting charcoal and twigs will work fine outside.

As you're kindling your fire, try to think about your internal feelings. Are you certain you have a passion for the types of qualities you wish to draw into your life? If so, now's the time to start thinking about how each one will make you feel somehow happier or more complete, or just less alone. It's okay to just want somebody to hold . . . or more.

With your fires blazing, both literally and figuratively, say:

My passion and desires rage within me this night.
To keep them from consuming me, I feed them the fuel they desire.

Raise some emotional energy and pick up one of the symbols with your projecting hand. Visualize what it's a symbol of (in a generic sense—imagine no particular faces, for instance!). Think of the first word that describes this need to you, such as "passion," and feel your little bit of emotional energy moving to your hand. Experience a mini-peak of sorts as you infuse the object with energy, and say:

Passion (or whichever word), come to me in the form of a lover.

Throw the object into the fire, seeing an aura of energy flash around it as the flames begin to consume it. It will be okay if the fire never wholly burns the object, by the way.

Repeat the process of charging, naming, and burning with the one or two other symbols you may have brought. Achieve a mini-peak each time, and recite the same line about the desired trait coming to you in a lover (substitute the name of the trait, obviously). Remember, no specific faces or people's names should enter your visualization process.

Look up, above the flames, and note something interesting: The little auras around the objects—the ones you saw flash—did not wink out of existence. Instead, they've become a sort of mist floating above the flames, right at the top edge of bearable heat.

Move your receiving hand well above the flames so that you feel the heat in a nonsingeing way. Wave this hand through the imagined spiritual mist (of whatever color you perceive). Feel the inflamed energy sinking into your hand and residing there. Say:

> *I draw these energies to me.*
> *And draw I shall, until these energies manifest my desired mate.*

Either put out the fire or let it burn out. Bury what's left of the objects, after the coals and embers have all cooled down.

Should you come across someone you think matches your spell criteria, use your receiving hand to dowse whether he or she is right for you. If this person is indeed the one, your sympathetically linked hand will give you a noticeable dowsing pull.

Just don't let that hand pull too close to the potential date . . . when you first meet.

Be Happy, It Won't Kill You

No one wants to talk about depression. Yet unpleasant sorts of melancholy can settle upon just about anyone. I say "unpleasant" to separate it from the pretend form of melancholy that people sometimes play at—and you know just what I mean if you've been to a club where everyone tries to out-attitude and out-do everyone else.

But seriously, true depression has a powerful effect, being almost a sinister form of libido. Often described as "sex drive," libido has been identified as the root of all sorts of behavior. Depression seems to have its own sinister form of drive, too. But since we can't really locate this poisonous thing—it's been called vitriol, interestingly enough—we're best off not trying to banish it. For this reason, I've designed a rite that attempts to reverse some vitriol by injecting countering, happy energy into the soul.

Despite the title of this book and the usual trappings associated with the community of Children in Black, remember: Being happy won't kill you. It's okay to be filled with joy in the darkness—that's why it's beneficial to identify and acknowledge when you're drawn to the life of nightkind, so that you can enjoy the benefits.

No one ever died from being happy, although more than a few have died from being unhappy. Whether sorrow leads someone to suicide, or builds to create serious health problems within, being unhappy most certainly can kill.

Combat unhappiness with a positive rite like this one, but if it gets to be too much, do seek professional help, too. Sometimes a rite like this will even help bring you to the right "help," as the universe takes the path of least resistance to getting you back on the right path.

Go outside and look for the darkest patch of night you can find. I mean this in every way. Make sure there's practically no light either on the ground around you, or contaminating the skies above. Pure night, both around and above you, is what you're after. A field, far away from lights, is ideal, but in a pinch a rooftop can work, as long as there aren't too many streetlights and the like around.

Bring a black taper candle, matches, and a small bag or pouch with you.

Put the candle in your receiving hand and reach out to the night, with arm extended and wick pointing away.

Do three quick clockwise rotations in place, knowing that the candle is moving through the thought-carrying network of night.

Stop suddenly and drop to a crouch. Say:

> *Chaotic emotions demand order.*

Feel the mild dizziness from the spinning that you did pass away.

Light the taper and say:

> *Connected to a universe of thoughts,*
> *this dark taper illuminates with even the covert truth.*

Take the lighted candle and prepare to use the unlit end as a giant writing instrument. If soil is below you, you will be carving words into the ground. If it is concrete upon which you stand, bits of the candle will be smearing or breaking off as you "write," which is fine, too—the candle thus becomes a sort of messy crayon.

Don't fear the dripping wax, which I must point out will sting your hand. The wax won't really burn your flesh, cooling a great deal before it reaches your skin. You'll be using the slight stings in your rite.

What will you write with the candle, and by its light? Think of everything that causes you pain, sorrow, unhappiness. Take your time to let images or abstract thoughts of each item come to you. As each distressing thought enters your consciousness, write a statement that embodies the exact *opposite* energy, even if it means you're imagining a better reality that isn't here yet (maybe you'll help bring it about). For example, should thoughts of your parents fighting trouble you, write, "My parents have peace, and they have love for me." You should try to keep your statements short, considering the obvious writing difficulty you might face after a while of candle dragging. Also, shorter statements help to drive the meaning into your subconscious with more force.

As you're going through this emotional brainstorming and spiritual housecleaning of sorts, the candle will occasionally shock you with its dripping wax. Let the sting reinforce the fact that, indeed, there is pain in your life. But think of the positive statement you're writing at the current moment, and how it can take away a bit of the pain. As you think this thought, the pain from the wax drop will disappear anyway, enhancing the symbolism of the rite.

When you've let out as much as you can in the form of statements, you may find yourself almost more agitated than at peace. Dredging up these memories, and constantly being stung by warm wax, will have built up some real frustrating energy.

Use it!

Stand up, raise some extra emotional energy (although you may be close to peaking anyway), and peak as you scream out the following:

Only what I wrote may be!

Drop suddenly, turn the taper over, and stick it into the soil or smash its top into the concrete. Either way, the goal is to put out the flame. Whisper:

Only what I wrote will be.

Pick the little wax droppings off your hand and put them into the bag or pouch you brought. Keep this bag with you and look at the wax drippings whenever you feel yourself sinking into despair. They'll remind you of the opposite side of reality you wrote about this night.

Don't worry about what you wrote. Leave the positive messages for the night. You should bury the candle.

Spells to Send Things Away

Banishing influences or most anything from your life is best done as the moon is decreasing in phase. Again, though, magickal needs wait for no lunar phase. If you need help right away, by all means, Witch, cast that spell and cast away any negativity that plagues you.

Stop Being Abused

Abuse is never pleasant, and can border from mildly irritating to illegal and safety-threatening. Should you find yourself in a situation in which you feel as if the police or another authority figure should step in, trust your intuition and turn to these people! It's okay to get powerful, physical help in such cases. Don't trust a rite to work quickly enough to prevent your life from coming to a violent end. Never trust that your magick is that "on." Calling on a cop or even a teacher can save the day!

But there is abuse that no police or other type of person can help with, either. If you're dealing with the annoying kind of pushing around that others turn their backs to, have I got a downright wicked little way to protect yourself. Some might call it sinister, but hey, they're not the ones getting pushed around. Besides, you'll see when you do it that there's no negative karma at play—at least, none of *your* negative karma.

This is the rite where I'll be recommending that you work with a particular deity. This Goddess is one of the three Greek Furies—the most aggressive one, Tisiphone. She is the one who can make sure that your bully becomes fully aware of the consequences of his or her negative karma. Think of Tisiphone as a karmic-payback accelerator.

Write an invocation to Tisiphone that asks for her help in rectifying the particular situation you find yourself in. Somewhere in your invocation, consider adding something to the effect of:

It is (name)'s own karma I seek to make him/her feel the effects of this night.

With your simple or true invocation done, proceed to act as the Goddess (a godform assumption will, of course, make this easier).

See, with your eyes open, the person who has wronged you. Make eye contact with this phantom form, and allow to swell within you plenty of the anger and hatred that you feel toward this person. As creepy as it sounds, being in the presence of the Goddess Tisiphone will seem to make it easy to let the emotions rise. But note that you're not raising this anger for reasons the casual observer would expect— critics, please bear with me a little longer!

When you feel the hate and anger almost consuming you with supernatural nausea, take a deep breath, raising some emotional energy. Hold the breath and will all your hate and anger to come out with your exhalation.

Exhale this cloud of hate and see it form into a brown mist in front of you, obstructing your view of the phantom foe you've imagined.

Try to just barely make out your bully moving a step or two back, recoiling from the hate cloud. Yet the cloud does not reach out to your foe or harm him or her in any way.

Command the cloud, with the will of the Goddess, saying:

All my hate for (name) I release to the dark ether.
Hate shall plague me no longer.
Yet night exacts a toll for the release of such agony.

See the cloud rise into the night, revealing a view of your bully. Feel nothing for him or her—no fear, no friendship . . . nothing. He or she is to be judged only by the Goddess.

Say to the person's phantom form:

In the name of Tisiphone, I summon your karma, (name).
May the weight of all the times you've wronged me
and others bind you from harming us again.
It is not we who have suffered at your words
and deeds who bring this upon you.
It is the nature of the balance and harmony that night seeks.
So mote it be.

Wave your projecting hand in the direction of the phantom, as if disregarding it. Say:

> *You have my pity, for at the moment of your strongest binding,*
> *you shall know why constriction overcomes you.*

Let the phantom vanish.

This rite is not to be taken lightly. It will work with eerie power to karmically bind your bully from harming you and anyone else ever again.

And this bully might even learn a lesson in the process. Supernatural bad luck has a funny habit of opening eyes, so to speak, as its effects are felt.

Lose Weight Safely

Supermodels, rock stars, and actors unconsciously set forth the idea that it's only acceptable to be rail-thin. And some people find it very hard to fit any ideal but the one set forth by pop culture. As a result, peer groups embrace said ideals, making it even harder for those who don't fit in. Not only may someone struggle with their own insecurities about weight, but may have to put up with teasing and worse things from others.

Realistically, you should only worry—and I mean seriously worry—about your weight when it has a chance of endangering your health. This includes not allowing yourself to get too heavy *or* too thin. The heart suffers from either extreme, and each gender has a slew of problems that can arise from going too far toward either end of the weight scale.

As with the rite for depression, this spell isn't designed to replace the possibility of necessary counseling. If you find that an eating disorder or obsession with your weight is preventing you from functioning normally, then by all means get help.

I don't mind admitting my own grim secrets from time to time if it means readers will find help. I've had bouts with eating disorders for years.

But I've done something about it.

Personally, I never went to counseling, opting to apply mystical techniques to get my eating disorder under control. Yet even once I got past that help phase of dealing with my problem, I still needed a way to stay thin, yet not launch into a depressing relapse of anorexia. As any therapist will tell you, an eating disorder, or the penchant for sinking into one, lingers, sometimes forever.

Whether you have an eating disorder or just want to drop a few pounds, consider controlling your weight with the mystical cheat that you're about to learn. Combined with some reasonably sensible food choices, it can help you find an obsession-free way of controlling how much you weigh.

Before you do the rite, however, begin by learning a little bit about sensible eating. Look into no silly fad diets, though! Research, instead, how many daily calories you need to maintain your weight for your height (one-third of these calories should come from fat). A little digging will show you what this daily total is, and even how to calculate roughly how many of the necessary nutrients are found in certain types of foods.

No need to become a computer, here. Just do some basic homework to determine what science recommends you eat to maintain your weight. Then try to find a calorie count that's a little lower, yet comfortable, so you can consider yourself eating "light." Even this light total may be more than you thought you'd be capable of having per day, and should be a positive as well as practical realization to begin your mystical working.

The point is, you can't eat tons of cake and french fries and expect this rite to work. You always have to work in league with any magick that you do. This spell will actually make it easier to eat properly, and will help you overcome the effects (mental and physical) of the few times when you do slip up.

Gaze into your nocturnal portal at an angle that lets you most clearly make out your reflection.

Concentrate on this somewhat transparent reflection of your face. See exactly what you dislike about the shape of your face. Note all the ways that you are displeased with how your weight makes your face look. It's actually okay to go overboard here, even finding fault with what never bothered you before. Such exaggeration will actually make a forthcoming part of the ritual easier.

When you've focused for about three minutes on every aspect of your face that you see or imagine as being too heavy, you're ready to try to "move" the reflection. Because the reflection is not crisp or vivid, looking more like an open-eyed visualization than a reflection, it should be possible for you to move the reflection into the air above the portal. See as best as you can with eyes open that your reflection is slowly sliding up and out of the portal, as if someone were moving a projector responsible for casting the image onto the portal.

Take your time to convincingly drag this exaggerated reflection into the air. When you feel that there really is a phantom version of your face there, say:

Behold how I wish to never be again.

Raise some emotional energy, especially drawing from any memories of times when your weight made you unhappy.

Now, peak the energy to your own physical face. Feel the peak rush up to your face, warming it. Blast that energy out of your face toward the phantom one.

See the emotional energy move as an orange cloud that your phantom face absorbs.

Imagine as best as you can that your own face now feels dry and itchy and warm. Trust me on this. Almost feel the skin on your face hurting from the sensation, if you can.

Got it? Good, because here comes the trickiest part.

Imagine that the phantom face is tightening and becoming ideally thin (make sure your ideal is healthy looking—no imagining a skull with a taut layer of flesh over it!). The tricky part is that, as you see the phantom face tightening, you should allow the itchy pain on your own face to morph into a sensation of tightening. You should feel almost as if a vacuum or black hole is being created inside your closed mouth. Sense a definite suction pulling the itchy skin inward. You'll note that the better you imagine the scratchy pain on your skin, the more realistic the inward pulling will feel (I'm not sure why, but this is definitely so).

As soon as the phantom face has completed visually morphing into one that you believe is perfect, reach out to it and grab it right away. Say:

Behold the face I shall wear from this night forth.

Pull the phantom face, like a mask, on to your physical face. Don't worry about the fact that it's oriented in reverse. You need the shock of seeing your ideal face flying toward you, literally head-on, as you pull it on.

Immediately feel how your face is energized and warmed by the experience. The tight feeling is still there, but some of the pain has gone away.

Raise some emotional energy, and do your best to have it all coalesce within your face. Sense this energy's presence as an orange sphere, glowing within your head. Then feel this energy from your face begin to spread down your neck, carrying with it the tightening feeling. Imagine the sensation moving down you, encompassed in the orange sphere. Imagine that each part it moves over is tightening, just as your face did. You will be surprised by how easy this is to imagine after you achieve it in your face.

Slowly move the sphere down, making sure to tighten every part of your body.

When you've tightened even your toes, raise some emotional energy and say:

May I achieve the ideal body I seek.
May my eating always work in accord with this need.
May I always think and be both thin and healthy.

Reach peak and say:

So mote it be.

Focus one last time on the tight feeling of your skin, and let the feeling gradually fade.

Eat intelligently, and repeat this rite every night for a month.

After just a couple of days of doing the rite, however, watch for how you feel in the morning. You should sense, upon waking, a touch of the tightness you imagined in the ritual, although it won't be quite so imagined!

After the month, you can switch to doing it once a week for a month, then just once a month. Should you no longer feel the need for it at some point, trust your instinct and discontinue for a while.

It's always an option when you feel the need to use it again.

Quit a Dangerous Addiction

I am definitely not capable of telling you, in a book, if you or someone close to you has an addiction. Sure, there are warning signs listed in all sorts of self-help books, but even those signs should really be accompanied by enough disclaimers to warrant a few appendices at least.

From what I've seen, it's impossible to judge whether someone is addicted solely by behavior, and especially if said behavior is only observed a few times.

Certain types of people try something a few times—even binge on it, perhaps due to their "extreme" personalities—and then quickly grow sick of it. Other types of individuals try something once and can never get enough of it again. Were you to observe either of these types of people indulging on a particular night, you'd incorrectly assume that both were addicted, when in fact only one is.

There's also the type of person who finds a thing he or she likes— say a favorite drink or a type of cigarette—and sort of sticks to it as an occasional social treat. Interestingly, some of these social drinkers or smokers can go virtually forever without ever having to up their intake ante. Year after year, they persist in having one drink, one cigarette, one whatever, whenever there's a party.

So it's difficult to classify by one's behavior whether he or she has an addiction. The only way to determine this is by the feelings associated with a need. And the only person who can honestly evaluate such feelings is the person with the potential problem.

If you suspect you might have a problem, first try to figure out which of the three general types best describes you. If you're extreme with everything you do, and extend this to substances, it can certainly lead to an addiction, and I'd be lying if I didn't say you were taking a risk—even if the risk is *just* lung cancer (other substances can kill more quickly, obviously). If you've recently tried something and now find yourself longing for it frequently after just that one taste, then danger might be coming. Verifying whether you're of the eternally in-control social type is hard to do without plenty of time and, equally, risk.

Obviously, the safest thing to do is avoid all dangerous substances. However, let's be realistic. The odds of never having a glass of wine in your life, for example, are pretty slim considering how ingrained in celebrations of all types alcohol has become.

I have no comment on how to handle illegal substances, by the way. They're dangerous and, well, illegal. Of course the only thing I can tell you is to avoid them.

Was that a disclaimer?

Anyway, unless you plan on living completely free of anything even remotely addictive—and I'm awed by those who can choose such a path—you'll have to make sure that you can spot addiction before it spots a weakness in you. It's necessary if you want to make sure you're always in control of your destiny, mindset, and actions.

If you feel something is beginning to get a hold of you, try this rite—right away! And act in accord with it. Stay away from the substance and see how you feel. Ideally, you'll stay away forever if the substance is something that has an unhealthy allure for you.

However, if you fall heavily into an addiction, you won't exactly be able to concentrate on achieving a magickal goal, either. And this isn't a rite that another Witch will be able to do for you.

For whatever reason, if you find that the rite is not alleviating your need, get help. It's nothing to be ashamed of, and sure beats the alternative.

Buy a pack of sterile lancets (the little needles that diabetics use to obtain a drop of blood for testing). You will also need to obtain a tiny sample of the substance that has you in a state of craving (an ounce of liquor or a cigarette, for example).

Place a small white washcloth (one you're willing to part with forever) on the altar. Rest the substance on top of the cloth and in a ready-to-use form, such as poured into a shot glass, lit and resting on an ashtray, or whatever makes sense. Make sure that the substance and its container are to the left side of the spread-out washcloth, so that a few inches of cloth remain to the right.

Get a pair of scissors and keep it handy.

Before you begin, thoroughly wash your hands with soap and water. Next, open the sterile lancet and hold it in your receiving hand. You will need to ready the pointer finger of your projecting hand to be eventually pricked during the ritual. To do such readying, pinch together your projecting hand's pointer finger and thumb, thereby squeezing the skin of your projecting pointer finger.

Move the sterile lancet so it's almost touching the squeezed finger, ready to strike.

Now, stare at the substance on your altar for a moment, and let yourself raise any feelings you have related to the substance. Why do you desire it? How did it make you feel the last time you enjoyed it?

Allow your face to slowly lower toward the substance . . . closer . . . closer.

Begin to raise some emotional energy, almost achieving a passionate welling of "love" for the thing. As odd as it sounds for a rite of this type, try to get close to peaking while focused on all your adoration for the substance.

Move almost close enough to touch the substance with your lips.

Then, at the precise moment of peaking, stab your squeezed finger and pull your face away from the substance. Say:

Only pain can come from this obsession I feel.

The shock of the pricking should have dissipated a lot of the energy you raised, but do let whatever energy is still present in you move to the finger. Will the energy to move into the drop of blood forming on your fingertip.

Squeeze a drop or two of your blood on the exposed part of the washcloth. The types of punctures that these lancets make tend to heal quite quickly. In fact, after you release the pressure or pinch, no more drops may form. If one drop does well up after you're done squeezing a couple out, disregard the new drop for the rest of the rite. You won't keep bleeding, trust me.

Using your receiving hand, dump a little bit of the substance onto the other end of the washcloth (if it's a cigarette, just put it out and smear some of the ashes from the tip).

Make certain that the stain or deposit of the substance does not touch the red blood splotches on the other side of the washcloth.

Now, pick up the scissors and slowly open them with your projecting hand, raising emotional energy as you do so. Position the scissors to make the first cut, then begin to slice the washcloth in half at the point that lies between the substance stain and your blood.

Continue to raise energy. Just before peaking, say:

> *Never shall these two substances meet again.*
> *My blood remains free of (substance name).*

Peak, make the first cut, and yell:

> *Free!*

Continue to cut the washcloth, never letting any of the substance get over to the side with your blood on it.

To truly finish the rite, you must do three things:

Burn the half of the cloth with the substance and bury it.

Bury, but don't burn, the half of the cloth with your blood someplace a good distance away from where you bury the remains of the substance half.

Act in accord. Willfully avoid the dangerous item, and see how much easier it will be to do so.

Okay, so there's a fourth thing to do, too:

Be proud of yourself for coming this far!

Chapter Fourteen

The Bag of Night

Night's ether only covers half of our world at any given moment, giving the inhabitants of the other half no way to access the mysteries and magickal potency of the darkness until the sun sets once again.

Or is that not quite true? If night is so tangible, mystically, shouldn't it be possible to keep some of it with us, at all times, much as a Druid can carry a sacred twig away from a grove?

Certain objects of power already in your possession have the essence of night in them. Your nocturnal portal is one; the obsidian from your initiation is another. Yet neither of these quite simulates the ability to reach out into the night and feel the tangible darkness.

To feel the palpable night by day, you'll need to create a mystical object that houses the very stuff of night. The idea for such a thing came to me when listening to night for inspiration on how to . . . well, on how to listen for inspiration and work dark magick better by day.

The occasional need to do such workings by day does arise, and I wanted a way to still get some of that nocturnal connection.

We'll call this object I literally daydreamed up the "Bag of Night" —a portable container of the dark ether. As you'll find when we get to its instructions for use, the bag can be slipped into most any ritual to make the mystical doable while that pesky sun is still high overhead!

While night will still always be a better time to work, the bag will help you bridge some of the gap between the ritual potency of night and day.

Creating the Object of Power

The bag is a pouch really, but "bag" is how it came to me in inspiration, so that's the name I'll continue to use for it. Physically, the Bag of Night is a black pouch of any size that you wish to forever dedicate to this purpose. There can be no color present—that includes the cord that you use to pull it shut. *"Black Only"* is the rule.

As far as specifications go, color (or the lack thereof) is the only real criterion. You might want to read the whole chapter before choosing a pouch, as the sample uses of it might help you determine what size and type you should be looking for in stores.

You can sew your own black pouch if you wish to make it fully a work of your own. I had no problem with buying one, being anxious to avoid sewing lately. I used a pouch that sort of made itself known to me in a Salem shop when I was visiting. For future reference, when you ask a store employee if he or she has something in stock, and are told no, but then the said item literally falls on you from an overhead shelf about ten seconds later, well, it might just mean you've found exactly what you're looking for.

Good thing I wasn't looking for an athame!

With your bag somehow selected, you'll need to make certain there isn't a speck of color outside or inside of it. Remove any little manufacturer label that might be present, and use a marker to cover up any color stitching that might show up. Of course, any decent manufacturer wouldn't dare ruin a perfectly good black pouch with white thread, but who knows?

To now turn this bag into an object of power, you should wait for the darkest night there is—the New Moon—and find the darkest place you can possibly work. For this rite, outdoors would be best.

Seriously. You're far better off doing this one outdoors.

Set up your altar as normal, but put the bag outside your circle, to the west. Make sure it is open as wide as possible, and even bent over sideways slightly, as if you were trying catch raindrops in the pouch's mouth.

Note that I'm not only recommending a particular Goddess to invoke for this rite, but I'm also giving the invocation. Meditate on what the words mean before you consider replacing them with your own. When you see what I'm going for, feel free to write it your way if you wish. While I always advocate that you write your own invocations, this is one that's pretty specific and actually the heart of the rite.

Also, do not set up a drink and treat for this rite. Trust me on this. You will want to move through the night afterward while still in a mildly altered state.

Activating the Bag of Night

Without ever looking at the pouch lurking in the shadows, do a banishing of some type.

Cast a magick circle, also trying to avoid a glance at the pouch as you move about.

If possible, do a full godform assumption of the Goddess Nyx. At the very least, imagine that you resemble her as you read an invocation. Use this invocation if you wish, or one that is similar:

> *Mother of Dark Gods, grant me the ability to move*
> *with the freedom that only the Gods possess.*
> *I seek to gather the matter of your robes,*
> *the very essence of your hair and skin, this night.*
> *Dark Mother, clothe me in night so that the shocks may not be too severe.*
> *For I seek to move between worlds, unscathed by the chaos that you once emerged from.*

In the presence of the Goddess, bask in her power for a moment and fixate on how it feels in comparison to your normal emotional energy. Try to raise more of this Goddess power through the same method you'd use to raise emotional energy. You should find it possible with almost no effort to have the energy you raise be that of Nyx. She is with you, after all.

Amidst the power of the Goddess' presence, you will not be able to accurately judge your peak level of energy. For this reason, don't try to peak. Let the peak come as a result of an action that you will be taking soon.

Begin to move clockwise around the altar, letting your arms move freely and chaotically as the Goddess may inspire you to do. Move a little farther away from the altar with each circumambulation. Feel the elation brought about by this ever-widening spiral dance of sorts, and let your energy level rise even higher.

When your spiral path brings you to the perimeter of your circle (after less than ten times around in all likelihood), make sure to stay within its confines and at the border for one complete circumambulation.

The next time you pass the west, do not allow yourself to make it quite to the north. Stop suddenly at some random northwest spot between those two quarters, and pivot counterclockwise so that you are facing the approximate location of the pouch. As you're not at the west quarter, the pouch will be a little distance from you.

Jump, leap, practically launch yourself out of the circle from this random northwest spot, being sure to direct your chaotic move toward the pouch. Don't worry if you land on it. It can be dusted off later. Just be sure to land within immediate reach of it.

The energy you'll feel at this point should be quite chaotic, but no harm will come to you.

Pick up the bag as quickly as you can, pivot clockwise, and look at your nocturnal circle/sphere. See how it looks from out here—a silver sphere with black mist clinging to it from the outside. Be certain to see it exactly in this way.

Take a couple of steps toward the circle, and with two hands hold the pouch open.

When you reach the west perimeter of the circle, take the pouch and touch it to the black mist pressing against the giant silver sphere. Make a slight swiping movement, catching some of the mist in the bag.

Begin to move clockwise around the outside of your circle, dragging the open bag along the perimeter. See more and more of the solid ether scraping off the circle and being forced into the bag.

After a complete circumambulation, pull the pouch tightly closed and say:

Nyx, with your help, my will has been done.
The darkness that emerged from the chaos is now housed within this Bag of Night.
So mote it be.

Hold the Bag of Night to your chest, raise some more emotional/Goddess energy, and jump into the circle.

Drop to a crouch, and relax for a moment.

Put the bag on the altar.

Thank the Goddess for being with you.

Close the magick circle.

Take a long walk in the night, if possible, keeping your bag in your pocket or in your hand. Feel how it moves through the night as one with it. It should almost seem weightless in your imagination.

Using the Bag of Night

What you've created during that somewhat unorthodox ritual is a powerful object, as you'll find. The nocturnal ether that you gathered in the pouch will never truly abandon it. The ether has become a part of the very darkness that the Bag of Night houses. Just never open the bag for fun. Treat it as a holy object of sorts.

When you need to open the pouch by day, from this point on you should only do so when you're inside at least a banished area, if not a full magick circle. And it will likely be daytime when you'll need the pouch, as night has its own ether to lend to your workings. If you want to open the Bag of Night at night, you can do so anywhere, as long as it's not for some mundane purpose.

You can also carry the bag, pulled tightly shut, with you at any time, day or night.

With these simple rules followed, what will this mystical object do for you? Again, it is something that houses the very essence of night. That is why it is actually a good idea to carry it around sometimes. It will help you remain open to more of the night-like bits of intuition that seem to fade during the day.

You can certainly also just leave the bag on your altar during any daytime rites, thereby lending them a bit of a nocturnal edge.

But the true power of this object, as I hinted at earlier, is its ability to let you simulate the feeling of reaching into the dark ether. Any time a rite needs you to somehow charge an object with energy, this bag can help.

Any of the rites that call for you to walk around the circle drawing in some of night's ether can be aided with the use of the pouch. How else could you work such magick in the daytime? Simply open the Bag of Night and slip one end of the object into it. Then, you could walk around the circle and know that the same type of nocturnal energy is building because of the sympathetic link to darkness inside the bag.

Other things to try include using the bag when listening for night's inspiration, by day. Make the room as dark as possible, and proceed as usual, being sure to start with a banishing. However, before you get to the point where you're ready to listen for or sense your answer or inspiration, open the bag and put it to your ear. This symbolic gesture and sympathetic link will help your current link to the information flowing through the dark ether.

And what about a boost for reading tarot? Consider putting the cards in the Bag of Night for a few moments and saying a few words about how they'll now be a better tool for seeing with clarity.

You can put any object that you want to magickally charge in the bag, in fact. Even some of the ingredients from the spells you learned in the last chapter can be put here first, then used in the rites.

Any time you desire the ability to touch the palpable ether of night, reach into the dark pocket. That inner space is sacred in that it was created to stand between worlds. Feel the fabric inside and know that the night, too, is just as real and solid for you at that moment.

But one important guideline to using the bag:

Do not send any energy of your own into it.

Do not, for instance, create a thoughtform and launch it into the bag. Think of the bag's inside as a small leak in the fabric of reality. The dominating dark ether will rush out of the Bag of Night any time you open it. Don't try to plug this up by pushing stuff back in. Let the energy come out, and use that energy in your rites.

Note that from time to time it will be a good idea to leave the bag open outside your circle, outdoors and at night, of course. While you are doing your ritual, the bag will get a bit of an extra boost from being in such a place at such a magickal time.

Unless you do something to destroy the sanctity of the bag—something like open it outdoors in the daytime and slip a pair of sunglasses into it—the bag should never again need the full ritual charging.

It will always be a link to the dark by day.

Chapter Fifteen

Strange Powers

With time and repeated magickal practice, most Witches begin to experience strange things happening even when they're not actively performing a spell or waiting for the results of one to take effect. As you might have noticed in your own life by this point, working with power can result in an overall boost in power.

The rites and techniques in this chapter are designed to help some of your natural abilities along, bringing them closer to the realm of supernatural ones. Closer, that is, to being true powers.

These powers you're about to experience and develop are not of the type you'll be using as mere interesting experiments or cool party or parlor entertainment. Rather, they will help your overall magick and work with energy, and one of them will even make it a bit easier to move around by night, as you'll literally see when you read on.

Dissolving Clouds

No secret to the ancients, energy can radiate from the eyes. The captivating gaze of legendary hypnotists is not all showmanship. In fact, your own gaze has likely become more magnetic not only as a result of your work on magnetism, but also from the boost your general confidence has received from increased magick use. All this makes you actually radiate, and the eyes are a place from where the power can be directed and focused.

You will come across many rites or even create ones in which it is most logical to direct the emotional energy present in your body to come out of your eyes. After all, your eyes are what you use to direct your attention toward something. It's natural to also use them to direct your will.

To enhance your ability at moving energy in this way, you can perform the following exercise, which happens to be a strange little power in itself. And a useful one at that.

Ever wish you could have a clear patch of sky to look at? Perhaps you wanted a better glimpse of the moon, but some pesky cloud was in the way? Maybe you wanted to draw on the chaotic pattern of the Milky Way stars for inspiration, but overcast skies left you unfulfilled?

Why not just blast the blocking clouds away then?

I'm not the first occultist to have noted that it's possible to use energy to destroy clouds. William Reich's work with Orgone energy (his name for emotional energy, or lifeforce) revealed how, with the help of a simple device, or "accumulator," one could do the feat, repeatedly. Several New Age paths have included forms of cloud-busting as a preparatory exercise.

Here's how to do it so it works without any tools, and how to do it in a way that will benefit all your energy-directing magickal workings from here on. Part of the basics of this technique will also help you carry out the night-vision rite that comes after.

Optical Streams of Energy

Find a spot outdoors at night where it is fairly dark, and where you will not be disturbed. Make sure, of course, that there are clouds in the sky. Pick a large cloud to gaze at, and make sure it is not too high up the horizon. You should never attempt to project your energy with your eyes tilted up (or down), so you'll need to find a cloud that's low enough to allow for a natural, comfortable head tilt.

Achieve some inner quiet, with your eyes closed and head tilted at the angle of the cloud. That is, if your eyes were open, you would be able to see the cloud straight ahead.

Open only your left eye and begin to gaze at the cloud.

Place your receiving hand palm over your closed right eye. Also, place your projecting hand palm against the back of the right side of your head, just behind the ear. In other words, if your head were not present, your hands would be able to come together and meet, palm to palm.

Still focusing on the cloud, raise a little emotional energy and direct it to your projecting hand. Imagine that a purple beam is coming out of that palm, passing through your head and closed eye, and being drawn into your receiving palm. Spend a few moments (but no more than a minute or so) really seeing and feeling that purple beam's presence, all while keeping your left eye fixed on the cloud.

Now, close your left eye, too, and move your receiving hand so that your palm covers the left eye. At the same time move your projecting hand to the opposite spot behind your head on the left side.

Open your right eye, and simply let it gaze at the cloud. Raise a little more emotional energy and direct it through your left, closed eye, seeing and feeling the same purple beam as before, for about another minute.

Close both eyes again, and remove your hands.

Turn your receiving hand sideways and keep your fingers together and extended. With eyes closed, position this flat hand, palm to your face, as if you are trying to cover both eyes with it. Keep it far enough from your face, though, so the hand is only touching the tip of your nose.

Raise approximately half of your maximum emotional energy level. Imagine that your entire body is tingling and glowing with the purple energy you imagined before.

Build to a peak, opening your eyes as soon as you get to this level.

Pull your receiving hand away suddenly, revealing the cloud to your view.

See and feel the purple energy fire up into the night sky as blazing beams of energy. See the light burn into the center of the cloud you chose. Concentrate on the intense feeling associated with the energy beams for about fifteen seconds, keeping up the visualization.

Then, let go of all that conscious effort. Keep your gaze fixed on the center of the cloud, but don't worry about seeing the purple light anymore. Just continue to gaze at the spot on the cloud, and wait patiently.

Only fill your mind with inner quiet, and wait.

The center of the cloud will evaporate. Stay put long enough and the opening will spread, dissolving the cloud entirely.

Interestingly, in time you will find yourself able to dissolve clouds merely by relaxing for a moment, raising a little emotional energy, and staring at a spot in a cloud. The individual eye stimulation and visualization, however, do wonders at first for developing this power, and you should stick with them for a couple dozen times at least.

Enhancing Night Vision

What better power or ability can there be for nightkind than that of night vision? There are obvious benefits such as just being able to see where you're going when heading out to that midnight New Moon ritual, and more subtle benefits such as easily catching sight of that bat or owl that has a sign to deliver to you.

No matter what specific benefit you can think of, the simple truth is if you plan on spending a lot of time in the shadows, being able to see your way through them is a terrific power to possess.

Using a combination of eye-relaxing techniques (first developed by Dr. William Bates just before the 1920s) and ritualistic techniques, along with some obvious natural supplements, I was able to vastly improve my night vision. It's the same simple regiment you're about to learn.

While you won't be able to read a book in a pitch black room with these techniques, you will find that your night vision will be startlingly clearer and even more . . . realistic? The latter is the best way to try and describe the sense that you are not only seeing more of what's there at a physical level, but that you are also picking up on etheric attributes of objects, thereby adding more presence to them.

Something you'll seriously have to see to believe!

Note that three exercises or rites make up the night vision regiment. You should try to do each of them at least once a day for a month. After this time you should notice results, and should be able to try a month of practice every other night. The next month, try once a week. By this point, you should be ready to consider it a truly occasional exercise, as your abilities will be impressive.

All along, make sure you get plenty of vitamin A, either by eating orange vegetables or by taking vitamin pills (which are the friends of all we urban folk who couldn't plan out a balanced meal if our lives depended on it). I recommend pills over vegetables, actually, because they ensure you're getting enough and not too much of the vitamin. Eating too many orange veggies will have you actually looking orange in time! Anyway, getting vitamin A in moderation is something you'll want to continue doing even when you're not actively training your night vision.

Exercise One

Begin by achieving some inner quiet in a dark room.

Open your eyes and put your hands together before you, palm to palm and fingers extended (pointing up), as if you were praying.

Move your hands apart about three inches. It is okay if it is too dark to see them clearly, just estimate the distance.

Raise a little emotional energy and feel it moving from the palm of your projecting hand to that of your receiving hand. Try to also see this happening. The energy is purple, as with the cloud-busting exercise.

Do not try to control the energy flow with your breathing. Just feel and see it moving from projecting to receiving hands, as it naturally wants to.

Bend your wrists at so they are at 45-degree angles, thereby bringing only your fingertips together. Do not bend your fingers, though. Your straight hands should be forming a sort of pyramid. Feel and see the energy forming a more tangible layer between your hands.

Now, turn your palms to face you, so only your middle and ring fingertips are still touching. Then, place the fingers of your projecting hand in front of those of your receiving hand. In other words, were you to spread all your fingers slightly, you'd have a grid of little diamonds. But do not spread those fingers; keep them together.

Feel how the connected finger backs and fronts are exchanging energy. See how the entire aura around your hands is glowing purple.

Close your eyes and move your palms toward you so that you cover both lids gently. You'll find that with your perpendicularly overlapped fingers, the palms are perfectly positioned to cover your eyes.

Feel how the vibration of purple energy is reaching your eyeballs at this proximity.

Raise more emotional energy (without peaking). However, do use pleasant thoughts to do so. Remember things that made you happy as you raise this energy, but try not to visualize these memories too clearly. Merely get into a terrific, relaxed mood as you raise this energy.

Hold this heightened energy level for as long as you can—at least five minutes, but eight or ten would be ideal (you can use a timer). Let your emotional energy be high, let your eyes relax behind the closed lids and covering palms. And, importantly, feel the vibration from the palms seeping through. This is a lot to focus on all at once, but you'll find it easy after some practice.

When you can hold this emotional energy level no longer, say the exact following phrases:

My eyes adjust to glimpse night's seen and unseen wonders.
This sight comes with inner peace.

Reach peak and pull your palms away suddenly.

Open your eyes and get ready for Exercise Two.

Exercise Two

Move around your dark room, keeping your eyes fixed straight ahead of you. Do not strain them, but don't let them move. Only your head may turn to get something in your sights.

Gaze directly at objects that you come across. Note how they look within the precise center of your field of vision—which consists of a two-inch circle at the point of your optical focus.

Each time you come across an object and focus on it with the tiny center of your vision field, say:

My eyes adjust to glimpse night's seen and unseen wonders.

And raise some emotional energy.

See how the object looks, then turn your head, not eyes (keep them straight), to move to the next object.

With each object you choose (go for at least five), repeat the affirmation and energy boost, and remember to only use a direct gaze with no eyeball movement.

Get ready to do Exercise Three.

Exercise Three

Go around the room in the same pattern that you did for Exercise Two, looking at the same objects in the same order as you did before.

However, this time you will not gaze at them and determine how they look. You will still keep your eyes focused straight ahead, but you will move your head more. Rather than gaze, you will move your head from side to side in a slow, swinging motion, allowing sight of the object to come in and out of your field of vision. To gauge how fast you should do such swinging, each arc, from side to side, should take about two seconds.

Move your head side to side like this for about a minute (around thirty swings) with each object. Note how vivid the object appears each time your swaying motion brings the object into direct line of sight.

At your moment of greatest pleasure with the results—when you finally realize with each additional object that you're seeing them better now each time you catch a glimpse—raise some emotional energy and say:

This sight comes with inner peace.

When this is done with the last object, try to spend some leisure time in the dark. Either a nighttime stroll or just some quiet time away from light would be fine.

Simple as they may sound, these three exercises will do wonders for your night vision. Just remember to find time to practice them nightly for the first month.

Sex Magick

Even though there are books dedicated to the subject, and there were occult orders dedicated to the practice, sex magick can be really simple to implement. The most important thing to remember is that it's the art of channeling the power of an orgasm in the same way you can channel and apply emotional energy.

Actually, it's not really an art. Sex magick is much more like a power—an ability you develop and can use at any time (any time you're being sexually stimulated, of course). So, even though you can consider what you're about to read to be a rite, it's really a core magickal power that you can apply during any night of your life.

Before we get to the how-to, however, let me point out the how-not-to. Despite what you may read in other books, take this bit of personal advice:

Do not perform sex magick for the purposes of achieving a sexual goal!

If you try to do so, you'll find that the act of sexually charging a sexual wish makes it impossible to separate the mystical energies from the desire. In other words, you'll never truly be able to release the desire as you would with a thoughtform. Doing a sex rite to wish for "getting lucky" over the course of the next night would keep you in a constant magickal loop, with your sexually charged desire fueling your sexual desire, which is trying to be busy fueling your desire for sex. As messy a mystical process as it is a sentence!

So, if what you're wishing for has anything to do with sexuality, use a different form of projecting for it. You'll have much better results, guaranteed.

Adding Sexual Energy to a Desire

Do some form of ritual that results in the creation of a thoughtform to accomplish a goal. That is, ideally the rite will have you "place" your visualized goal into a ball of energy that you fire off into the ether or astral plane, where it may begin manifesting. Keep in mind that you can modify most any spell to result in such a charged, visualized ball of energy.

Make sure you visualize this thoughtform in your ritual as having a concrete, positive image associated with it. If you're wishing for health, see yourself as already healthy, and see this image floating inside the glowing sphere when you create it.

Do this no earlier than twenty-four hours before having a sexual encounter (it could even be a planned encounter with yourself; the only requirement is that there be a release).

During the initial phases of your sexual encounter, proceed without thinking much about the thoughtform.

After you're well on track to some activity that will result in you sexually climaxing, however, raise a mini-peak of emotional energy and will a mental connection to the thoughtform you created. Command it, quickly and silently, to be ready to receive its final boost of energy.

When you feel yourself about to climax, see the thoughtform floating somewhere to your side, as close to your groin area as possible.

As you begin to climax, see and feel a small white ball of energy leave your groin center and fire into the thoughtform.

Lose yourself in the climax and forget about the thoughtform, thereby releasing it and its energy boost to the ether.

The ability to send that first bit of sexual energy into a thoughtform, which already exists on the astral plane, is the real power requiring mastery here. Once you get the hang of it, you can apply that extra energy boost to achieve some very tangible results.

Only charge a particular thoughtform with sexual energy once, though. After this point, it should be strong enough to be manifesting at an accelerated rate. Trying to call it to your bed for another boost in the future would be difficult and possibly detrimental, keeping the form from doing its work.

Remember not to do sex magick for sex, and, also, do not tell your partner what you're doing unless he or she wants to help with charging the thoughtform. A lover who's not into the idea of sharing his or her time with you *and* magick might damage your thoughtform with a negative one of his or her own. Worse, he or she might make sure you're not going to get a chance to make two-person form of sex magick work that night.

Ah, what strange powers a lover can have over your immediate destiny!

Chapter Sixteen

Opening the Gates to the Underworld

The rite you're about to read may be used to literally grant you access to the Underworld—to the mythical representation of the afterlife. However, the first time I tried opening the gates to that realm, the Goddess Inanna had something else in mind for me. The Goddess whose form I had assumed in the rite took control of the rite, changing it and bringing to me a very different experience.

There is a chance that if you choose to perform this rite you, too, will not end up communicating with the dead. The Goddess invoked might decide to share, instead, a glimpse of your own dark half, in the form of a visible manifestation in your room of the Goddess Ereshkigal. And she will, curiously, look a lot like you do!

Either way, of course, you're in for the most powerful type of experience: seeing the unseen. Whether it results in the specter of a lost loved one or a life-changing confrontation with your dark inner self, this rite will leave you feeling never quite the same way about the occult world after you perform the unique steps involved.

I designed this rite to closely mimic the myth of Inanna's descent to the Great Below. I wanted it to be a psychodrama that made it easier to access the afterlife by mind communication. And, as I found, I had assumed correctly that the power of the myth had built up a tremendous thoughtform over the ages, and that tapping into it would have noticeable effects. Since performing it the first time, when Ereshkigal appeared before me, I've used the rite several times as a powerful and quite enchanting way to establish communication with the dead.

Note that the form of the ritual you will be reading here will not be the form that my first attempt ended up taking. That was controlled, mostly, by Inanna's godform, and I couldn't recall the changes she made exactly and put them down on paper if I tried. However, if you find the Goddess taking over and putting words into your mouth, or guiding you to add or modify actions, go with it!

Because of the tangible nature of what you'll see and hear in this rite, I've saved it for last, figuring it will be a powerful cap to this dark grimoire.

As you'll have no way of knowing if Ereshkigal will make an appearance in this rite, you'll need to have another purpose for doing it. That is, you should really only undertake this bit of elaborate necromancy if you have a deceased person in mind with whom you wish to communicate. For best results, you should consider trying for someone you knew personally and loved. They're more likely to make the etheric reach out to you, as well.

Just be realistic about what you expect from afterlife communication. The dead can never be a part of our living life again . . . in this incarnation. We do have the chance of some limited conversation, but that may not happen either if the soul we're calling has already reincarnated.

Setting Up

You won't need a photo of the deceased to perform this rite, although it would help to spend a few moments gazing at one before you begin.

Remind yourself of what this person was like, and build up some sensation of missing him or her (although that feeling might always be present in you if he or she passed on recently).

You will need some special components to make the rite work. It requires far more physical setup than anything you've become used to with the workings found in this book. I'll assume you haven't read the myth of Inanna's descent in describing what's needed, although you might want to check out the story in its best translated form (*Inanna*, by Diane Wolkstein and Samuel Noah Kramer, Harper & Row, 1983).

The rite simulates how Inanna was stripped of the seven *me* to be allowed access to the Underworld. This Sumerian word, *me*, is used to describe many types of attributes, but in this case it means some spiritual gift, trait, or object of power—things that make the Goddess even more powerful, in other words. The guardian of the Underworld and Ereshkigal's beau, Neti or Nergal as he's been called in different eras, is told by his love to take the seven *me* from Inanna before she'll be allowed entry. This was done as a symbolic trade for opening each of the seven gates to the Underworld, and it's implied that Ereshkigal asked for the *me* so that she could have power over her sister when she entered the Great Below.

We won't get into the myth's many possible interpretations, focusing instead on how the simulated removal of the *me* does have a powerful effect. While you're never really making yourself powerless, and never leave the circle or lose the presence of the Goddess within you, by simulating her actions you only make her own access to the Underworld more real to you. If she can open the gates, so can you, and that is what you will do!

Now, you'll need to simulate the seven *me*. In the myth, these items are listed as:

I. A crown;

2. a necklace of lapis beads;

3. a chest-worn double-strand of lapis beads;

4. a breastplate;

5. a gold bracelet;
6. a lapis measuring rod and line;
7. and a royal robe.

Note that the actual items do not have a significant amount of power. The reason they ended up in the myth, and eventually in this rite, is because they were physical attributes that the Sumerians recognized the Goddess as bearing in various inspired descriptions of her.

You will only need to *simulate* the seven items! There is no need to spend a few thousand dollars trying to create a royal outfit for the rite.

For the crown, anything from a headband you manufacture to some type of hat you own will work. You will need to bless this and all the other simulated *me* using a simple dedication you may have learned. You can even modify the dedication given in this book for the tarot, substituting the words to reflect each of the *me*.

For the lapis items, your best bet is to find a New Age store that sells little bits of the stone. Make a simple necklace with one or more such fragments, and a simple breast or chest pin with other pieces. These two items, respectively, will be the second and third *me*. The sixth, the lapis measuring rod and line, you'll note, sounds extravagant. You can just take a natural wand such as a short tree branch, and tie another simple lapis necklace to it, dangling from one end. It will look odd, which is perfect for telling your subconscious that something unusual is about to happen.

The breastplate, bracelet, and royal robe can be reusable items. After the rite, you can either choose to put them aside for repeating it, or use them in your daily life and just recharge them or others for use. For a breastplate, it's fine to substitute everything from a vest to a mock-turtleneck dickey. It just has to be something that covers, predominantly, only your chest. When you "suit up" during the rite, you will pin the chest pin to this, as the pin will be removed first.

The gold bracelet could be just that, although a silver or costume jewelry bracelet will work fine.

The robe can be a special ritual robe you have set aside, or a special outfit that you feel signifies to your subconscious the act of being dressed up, so to speak. Make sure you have nothing on underneath, as you will need to be completely free of all clothes at the final point of the stripping away segment of the rite.

In addition to these things that you will be wearing, you will need to set up an extra altar at the west quarter of your circle. Even though the Sumerians often referred to death as "entering the east," the connections you've likely built to the west gate as that of death will be stronger in the modern day and better for you to work with.

The west altar can be a simple box covered in a black cloth. On it should be at least some suitable representation of Neti. A statue of a soldier or even of some kind of dragon or guardian beast will do. Make sure there's plenty of room on this second altar, as you'll be putting all the *me* onto it during the rite. Also, if you can, paint a silver door (a simple upright rectangle will do) on the part of the black cloth that faces to the east.

Place the drink and treat just outside the circle, beyond this west altar.

Set up your main altar as usual. Do consider that you will be invoking the Goddess Inanna. Perhaps obtain a statue or other visual connection to her and place that on the altar.

You might want to copy the ritual on to index cards and place these in appropriate spots where the ritual will take you. Read through the rite a couple of times to determine which cards should go on which altar and which ones should go in the bathroom (for after the ritual bath, which we'll cover in a moment). Note that the words of the ritual are extremely important. While many rites are flexible, this one is designed to pull on many of the words actually sung and chanted about the Goddess thousands of years ago. Even though they're given here in English, the patterns of the words still have cosmic, unconscious power. They are legends that have been resonating, and you will be tapping into them better by not improvising.

The final preparation you'll need to make is to put all seven *me* in your bathroom and take a ritual bath. Light some candles, relax, and

meditate on whom you wish to contact. You might want to have his or
her picture on the edge of the tub to contemplate.

After your bath is done and you are dried off, you can begin.

Opening the Gates to the Underworld

Standing naked, try to achieve some inner quiet.

Say:

With awareness of the Great Above, I turn my attention to the Great Below.
In moments I will be one with Inanna, approaching the Great Below.
I adorn myself with the seven me, preparing for the Great Below.

Put on the "robe," then the "breastplate" that you chose. Add the necklace and pin, then the bracelet.

Place the crown on your head, then pick up the lapis-adorned rod.
Say:

I set out for the Underworld.

Walk out to the room where your two altars are set up. Make sure that
the only lights present after you enter the room are the candles on the
main altar. The rest of the room should be as black as possible.

Perform a banishing.

Cast a magick circle, but instead of using your athame to do so, use
your wand with lapis dangling from it.

Invoke the Goddess Inanna, assuming her form as best as you can.
Use the following words to make your invocation:

From the Great Above, Inanna,
be with me as I turn my ear to the Great Below.
From the Great Above, Inanna,
join me now so that I may open the gates to the Great Below.
Queen of Heaven and Earth, with these seven me do I hope to honor your presence.
Great Mother Inanna, it is with your support
that I now descend into the kur, into the Underworld.

Turn 180 degrees counterclockwise, in place, and walk toward the altar
you've set up inside the circle, to the west.

Use the base of the wand (not the end with the string hanging
from it) to knock loudly on the altar of the west. Say with intensity:

> *Open the door, gatekeeper.*
> *Open the door, Neti.*
> *The Goddess Inanna would now enter.*
> *The Queen of Heaven approaches the west.*

Imagine that Neti is present just beyond this altar, lurking in the darkness. Visualize him as your instinct guides you to do—even skry for a glimpse of him in the darkness, if it helps.

When you feel his presence on some level, move away from Neti, completing one counterclockwise circumambulation around your circle.

Return to the west, and raise a little emotional energy to one of those mini-peaks you're familiar with by now.

Take off your crown, place it on the west altar, and say:

> *I enter the first gate by surrendering my crown.*
> *The ways of the Underworld are perfect and may not be questioned.*

Move counterclockwise around the circle again and achieve another mini-peak of energy when you return to the west.

Remove your necklace, place it on the west altar, and say:

> *I enter the second gate by surrendering my bead(s) of lapis.*
> *The ways of the Underworld are perfect and may not be questioned.*

Go around the circle counterclockwise, return to the west, and do a mini-peak.

Take the pin off your breastplate, place it on the west altar, and say:

> *I enter the third gate by surrendering my bead strand.*
> *The ways of the Underworld are perfect and may not be questioned.*

Make another counterclockwise circumambulation and achieve a mini-peak.

Remove your breastplate, place it on the altar, and say:

> *I enter the fourth gate by surrendering my breastplate.*
> *The ways of the Underworld are perfect and may not be questioned.*

Go counterclockwise around the circle and do another mini-peak of emotional energy.

Take off your bracelet, place it on the altar, and say:

> *I enter the fifth gate by surrendering this circle of gold (or silver).*
> *The ways of the Underworld are perfect and may not be questioned.*

Move counterclockwise around the circle and achieve a mini-peak when you return to the west.

Place your wand on the altar, and say:

> *I enter the sixth gate by surrendering my measuring rod and line.*
> *The ways of the Underworld are perfect and may not be questioned.*

Begin building a large amount of emotional energy. Keep raising this energy as you make an intense counterclockwise circumambulation. When you reach the west again, you will need to be close to a full peak of energy (but don't peak as soon as you arrive at the west).

Pull off your robe as intensely as you can, and throw it onto the west altar. Without peaking, practically yell:

> *I enter the seventh gate by surrendering my robe.*
> *The ways of the Underworld are perfect and may not be questioned.*

Imagine that a giant eye is staring at you from the darkness. See it as clearly as you can. It is okay if it makes you afraid. Go with whatever emotion wells up in you.

Put your hands behind your back and drop to your knees with the west altar before you. Scream as loud as you can to release and peak! ("As loud as you can," of course, implies you might have to simulate a scream with a powerful, falsetto whisper if there are others in the house.)

See the giant eye before you close.

Close your own eyes and let whatever feelings that are present rush through you.

Open your eyes and begin to skry the darkness that is before you. Issue the following command to the abyss:

> *As the Goddess was left a corpse, I am now among the dead.*
> *As the Goddess was left hanging as a rotting piece of meat,*
> *I find myself in the hall of the dead.*
> *Ereshkigal, grant me the sight of (name of the deceased).*

It is not I, but your naked and bowed-low sister who demands this sight.
For before Inanna rises, taking me away from this place, I demand sight of (name).

Continue to truly skry the darkness before you.

The deceased soul whom you are calling will appear and communicate with you, as long as he or she is still in the afterlife.

When the communication ends—such contact experiences rarely last longer than a few moments, sometimes minutes—close your eyes and raise a little emotional energy. Say:

With the offering the Goddess has made to you, Ereshkigal,
I am now free to take leave of this place.
For the time being, I am free of the hall of the dead.
Yet no one leaves the Underworld unmarked.
Dark Goddess, I am forever changed, and forever aware of the true unseen.
Forever aware of the Great Below.

Allow your hands to come forward from behind your back, and stand up slowly.

Begin to make seven clockwise circumambulations. Each time you pass the west, you should pick up one of the *me* and put it on again. You should do this in the reverse order of how you surrendered the objects, now reclaiming robe, then rod, bracelet, breastplate, bead pin, necklace, and finally, on the last circumambulation, crown. Each time you reclaim an item, say:

I close the seventh (then sixth, fifth, and so on) gate.

After your seventh time around, when you announce that you have closed the first gate, pivot clockwise to face your main altar. Walk to it, empowered.

Thank the Goddess for being with you, in your own words.

Close the magick circle.

One change to how you normally end rites, however: Do not go and partake of the drink and treat outside the circle. These should be poured and left outdoors to the westernmost part of your yard. These are an offering to the dead.

Remember, the rite might not play itself out quite the way it is written here. If the Goddess takes over, go along for the experience.

Whether such a confrontation with Ereshkigal happens in this rite or not, however, you are empowered by all your efforts on this path to face your dark half each night that follows in this incarnation.

Darkest blessings, Nocturnal Witch.